California Cookbook Company Presents

A Taste of MEXICO

Mexican, Southwest and TexMex Favorites

▼▼

Compiled By
**Professional Home Economics (FACS) Teachers
of California, Nevada, Arizona, and Utah**

Editor
Gerry Murry Henderson

Graphic Design, Typography, and Production
Mike Burk Production Services, Long Beach, CA

Visit us on the web at
www.californiacookbook.com

Library of Congress Catalog
Card No. 83-072751
ISBN 0-914159-13-5

A Taste o MEXICO

Thank you for purchasing A Taste of Mexico. ***This helps support vital programs in schools throughout California, Nevada, Utah, Arizona and Oregon. Each recipe has been generously donated by Home Economics and Family and Consumer Science Teachers,***

We have many people to thank for their part in producing this book and getting it distributed to hundreds of schools:

Grady Reed has been the owner and creator of California Cookbooks for over 25 years. His vision, inspiration and leadership have set a professional standard in cookbooks and fundraising. It has been his attention to detail and absolute dedication to customer service that has made this company what it is today; a provider of quality books and a simple way to raise funds for schools. *Thank you Grady!*

Nancy Freeman, our office manager for fifteen years, always does her job with a wonderful attitude. She handles customers, salespeople, delivery persons and takes care of all the office details with efficiency and a smile.

Gerry Henderson teaches Home Economics full time at Temple City High School and carefully edits each recipe.

Mike Burk designs our covers and inside photos. He takes the recipes and makes them into the quality books we are so proud of.

Delta Printing, in Valencia, along with **Jerry Bernstein,** makes sure the books are printed professionally and best of all, on time!

Roger Upperman, Robert Mauthe, Ron Rouintree, and **Danny Hawes** organize all the pick-ups of books from our schools and drive thousands of miles to give each teacher great customer service.

Eric Erdmann, Tim Campbell and **Marc Trimble** present these books to students in their classrooms, helping teachers kick off a successful sales drive.

Our photography has been donated by **Lawry's Foods, Inc., National Cattleman's Beef Association, American Sheep Industry, Dole Foods, Pillsbury, USA Rice,** and the **Wisconsin Milk Marketing Board.**

As we transition the company to new ownership, we will continue to provide quality cookbooks for the consumer and excellent service to our teachers who work hard to improve their programs.

Sincerely,

Doug Herrema and Doug Pierce

Owners California Cookbook Company, Inc.

P.S. Please note the **re-order form** on page 159.

P.P.S. You can also visit us on the web at: **www.californiacookbook.com**

TABLE OF CONTENTS

ON OUR FRONT COVER:
Ensenada Fish Tacos, page 110
Compliments of Lawry's Foods, Inc.,
www.lawrys.com

Professional Home Economics (FACS)
Advisory Committee

We would like to thank the following special people for their advice, ideas and support for this book...

KATHIE BACZYNSKI
Mt. Carmel High School, San Diego

PRISCILLA BURNS
Pleasant Valley High School, Chico

JAMIE DAVIS
Redwood Intermediate School,
Thousand Oaks

CAROLE DELAP
Golden West High School, Visalia

PEG ELLINGTON
Yucca Valley High School, Yucca Valley

PAM FORD
Temecula Valley High School, Temecula

MARIA FREGULIA
Lassen High School, Susanville

DEBBIE HARVEY
Amador Valley High School, Pleasanton

LA RAE HARGUESS
Hesperia High School

GERRY HENDERSON
Temple City High School, Temple City

GRACE HIBMA
Office of L.A. County
Superintendent of Schools,
Consultant Consumer
& Homemaking Education

CAMILLE HICKS
Riverton High School, Riverton, UT

NANCY HUNYADI
Fullerton High School, Fullerton

REIKO IKKANDA
So. Pasadena Middle School, So. Pasadena

DOTTI JONES
Etiwanda High School, Etiwanda

MARY LASH
Paramount High School, Paramount

JERI LUNDY
Grossmont High School, La Mesa

JAN MARTIN
Reed High School, Sparks, NV

ANN PORTER
San Luis Obispo High School,
San Luis Obispo

BETTY RABIN
Sierra Vista Jr. High School, Canyon Country

APRIL ROSENDAHL
Chino High School, Chino

KAREN TILSON
Poly High School, Riverside

MARIANNE TRAW
Ball Junior High School, Anaheim

SONJA TYREE
Ayala High School, Chino Hills

BETTY WELLS
Bidwell Junior High School, Chico

KATHRYN P. WHITTEN
Home Economics Education, Fresno

Introduction

Mexican food is fiesta food–casual, colorful, distinctive and fun.

You will enjoy discovering the rich culinary traditions of Mexico and the neighboring Southwestern portion of the United States. The cuisines of Mexico and the Southwest are built upon staples such as corn, tortillas, beans and chiles. The roots of American Southwestern cooking can be traced back to the pre-Hispanic area of Mexico.

Mexican Food & Nutrition

The Mexican diet is largely based on healthy carbohydrate foods, such as beans and corn. Beans are high in fiber and vegetable protein. Corn is processed into hominy, cornmeal and masa, a dough used in many dishes including tortillas, the bread of Mexican cooking. When corn, beans and vegetables are combined in a meal they compliment each other nutritionally, creating a valuable source of protein.

Seasonings give Mexican food its special identity. Chiles are low in calories and a good source of vitamins A and C, plus iron, magnesium, niacin, thiamin and riboflavin. Chiles are believed to increase the rate of calorie burn.

Hot, spicy cuisines traditionally tend to have a high salt content. The cuisines of Mexico and the Southwest, however, achieve their wonderful flavors through the use of chiles, spices, herbs, vinegars, lemon juice and lowfat condiments.

Fat-free tortillas for filling and rolling can be prepared by heating them on a hot griddle a few minutes until hot but not smoking. The tortillas will soften and become pliable. Left on the griddle for a longer period, the tortillas become lightly crisped. The tortillas can also be heated in the microwave, wrapped in damp paper towels and heated on high (5 tortillas per 30 seconds) or in the oven, wrapped in foil and heated at 350 degrees for about 15 minutes. Make low calorie chips by baking tortilla wedges on a baking sheet in a 350 degree oven for about 10 minutes.

Replacing sour cream, cheese and refried beans with reduced fat or fat free products now available in your grocery store can reduce fat and calories further. Leaner cuts of beef and pork are lower in fat. Chicken and seafood are also good choices for lowfat, low calorie meals.

About Chiles

Chiles are a cornerstone of Mexican and Southwestern cooking. Valued as a lively heat source for foods, they are also a good source of Vitamins A and C.

Capsaicin, a crystalline chemical, is the substance in chiles that causes the burning sensation in your mouth. In spite of the discomfort, the taste is addictive. Capsaicin is a digestive stimulant and promotes perspiration to cool down the body, which is important in hot climates such as Mexico and the American Southwest.

Capsaicin is concentrated in the seeds and white membranes to which the seeds are attached. Remove them to tame the chiles' firepower. *Wear disposable gloves while cutting chiles;* the oils can be very irritating. After handling chiles, rinse hands with water and salt, then wash with soap and water.

Popular Chiles

Cayenne Pepper
Intensely hot-dried Asian, Mexican and Louisiana varieties are processed into hot ground red pepper. Substitute ¼ teaspoon ground cayenne for one small, hot dried chile.

Crushed Red Chiles
These are the red chile flakes and seeds you find in shakers in pizza parlors. One small, hot dried chile is equal to 1/2 teaspoon crushed red chile pepper.

Chile Powder
Markets carry chile powder blends with added seasonings. To grind your own, heat 2 to 3 dried red New

Mexico chiles on a baking sheet in a 350 degree oven for 5 minutes. (Do not let chiles darken or they will taste bitter.) Discard stems and cool. Remove seeds for a milder taste.

Grind chile pieces in an electric spice grinder or coffee mill. One large dried, red chile equals about 1 tablespoon powder.

New Mexico Chile (chile verde)
Long green or red fresh New Mexico and Anaheim chiles are from the same pod variety. New Mexico chiles are hotter. They are interchangeable in recipes using large green chiles.

Fresh or frozen chiles have the best flavor and texture. Or, substitute flame-roasted, mild canned chiles and rinse before using.

Poblano
Blackish-green fresh chile that is similar to a bell pepper, only smaller. It has a broader stem base and triangular shape. Hotter than the Anaheim with a deeper, more complex flavor.

A top choice for stuffing, they're available fresh in the spring and fall.

Jalapeño
This 2-4" fresh chile is loved for its flavor and raw heat.

Serrano
Smaller, thinner than the jalapeño. A serrano heat-wave builds gradually, then engulfs the palate.

New Mexico Red (chile Colorado)

This dried variety includes Anaheim and California red. They produce an outstanding reddish to orange chile powder. Their heat ranges from mild-sweet to hot. These attractive chiles are strung to make colorful ristras.

Ancho

Reddish brown ancho is the dried, wrinkled form of the fresh poblano. Popular in Mexico and makes superior chile powder (called pasilla chile powder in California.) The sweet, rich earthy taste is preferred in Mexican red sauces.

Chipotles

Dried, smoked red-ripe jalapeño. It is quite popular.

Habanero

The hottest of all chiles!

Glossary

Burrito

Stuffed, rolled large flour tortillas.

Chilaquiles

Strips of stale, fried tortillas layered, most often with chile sauce. Luxurious versions include meat, cheese, tomatoes and onion.

Chimichanga

A specialty of Arizona, the chimichanga is a filled, folded burrito which is deep-fried and served with toppings.

Enchilada

These filled, rolled corn or flour tortillas are assembled in a casserole dish and baked in a sauce with melted cheese. Sometimes, enchiladas are stacked like pancakes and layered with filling.

Fajitas

Marinated grilled beef, chicken or pork that is thinly sliced and wrapped in flour tortillas with bell peppers, onions and seasonings.

Quesadilla

Two flour tortillas stuffed with cheeses and sometimes meat and vegetables, then cooked on a griddle.

Taco

In Mexico, tacos are made from corn tortillas, stuffed, rolled and eaten out of hand in a soft version, or slightly fried until crisp and chewy. Only in Tex-Mex cuisine are the tortillas folded and fried into crisp shells.

Tostadas

Tortillas which have been fried into a crisp, flat disc. They are covered with layers of beans, meat, cheese, lettuce, salsa, etc.

APPETIZERS & BEVERAGES

Baked Brie With Jalapeño Sauce

Serves 8

  2 (4 ounce) packages crescent roll dough
  1 (8 ounce) wheel brie cheese
  2 tablespoons jalapeño sauce
  1 egg, beaten

Preheat oven to 375 degrees. Work crescent roll dough into a circle large enough to completely wrap the brie. Place brie in center of dough. With fork, poke top of cheese several times. Slowly pour 1 tablespoon jalapeño sauce over top of cheese, allowing it to sink into cheese. Add remaining jalapeño sauce, poking cheese a few times more with fork (some sauce will run over the sides). Fold dough over top of cheese, working it together. Brush edges with beaten egg to seal. Bake 10 minutes, following directions on crescent roll package. Do not overbake. Serve immediately with crackers. Note: You may substitute phyllo dough (puff pastry) for the crescent roll dough.

"Try this recipe from our local paper, Stockton Record.*"*

Darlene Lupul   **Tokay High School, Lodi, CA**

Ceviche

Serves 6

1 1/2 pounds firm, white-fleshed fish
1 cup lemon juice
juice of 3 limes
2 tomatoes, peeled, diced
1/2 cup green onions, chopped
2 mild green chiles or 1/2 can (2 ounce) can green chiles, diced
1 teaspoon salt
1 teaspoon cilantro
1/2 teaspoon ground pepper
1/2 teaspoon garlic, mashed
1 teaspoon oil
4 stuffed green olives, diced
Garnish: 1 to 2 avocados, peeled and sliced, 2 to 3 tomato slices, whole black olives.

Cut fish into 1/2" pieces and marinate in lemon and lime juices until "cooked", about 6 hours, in refrigerator. Be sure fish has turned white (opaque). Don't leave in juice too long or fish will get "tough". Drain and rinse fish with water. Mix fish with remaining ingredients (except garnishes). Top with desired garnishes and serve with chips or crackers.

"My good friend, Janis Rodriguez, shared this recipe with me.
It's one of my favorite appetizers."

Pat Hufnagel   **Esperanza High School, Anaheim, CA**

Cheese Roll Olé

Makes 4 rolls

2 1/2 cups flour
1 cup butter, softened
1 cup sour cream
seasoned salt, to taste
cayenne pepper, to taste
3 cups cheddar cheese, shredded
paprika, for garnish
salsa, for serving

In mixing bowl, combine flour, butter and sour cream; mix well. Divide into 4 parts. Wrap in plastic wrap and chill until firm. Roll each part of dough out into a 12" x 6" rectangle. Sprinkle each rectangle with seasoned salt, cayenne pepper and 3/4 cup shredded cheese. Starting at the long side, roll up, jelly-roll fashion and seal ends. Place seam side down on an ungreased cookie sheet. With sharp knife, cut halfway through every inch. Sprinkle with paprika. Bake at 350 degrees for 30 to 35 minutes. Serve with salsa.

"Serve straight from the oven—melts in your mouth!"

DeLisa Davis   **Sutter High School, Sutter, CA**

Chile Cheese Empañadas

Makes 3 ½ dozen

> 1 package pie crust mix, double crust size
> 2 ½ cups cheddar cheese, shredded
> 1 (4 ounce) can green chiles, whole
> 1 egg white, slightly beaten

Prepare pie crust as directed; blend in 2 cups shredded cheese. Divide pastry in half and set aside. Remove seeds from chiles; cut into ½" x 1" squares. Roll out half of pastry on lightly floured board to 1/16" thickness. With cookie cutter, cut 2 (½") circles. Moisten edge of each circle with egg white; place a piece of chile and ¼ teaspoon shredded cheese in center. Fold in half, pressing edges together with a floured fork. Put on greased baking sheet; refrigerate or freeze. Continue with remaining half of dough. When ready to bake, brush with egg white and bake at 400 degrees for 12 minutes, until lightly browned.

"This is a favorite recipe of mine! I got it years ago from a PTA friend!"

Carolyn McBride   **Arcadia High School, Arcadia, CA**

Cinnamon Tortilla Chips With Strawberry Salsa

Serves 8 - 10

> *Tortilla Chips:*
> 8 large flour tortillas
> water
> ¼ cup sugar
> 2 teaspoons cinnamon
> nonstick cooking spray
> *Strawberry Salsa:*
> 2 Granny Smith apples
> 2 kiwi fruit
> 1 medium orange
> 1 (10 ounce) package frozen sweetened strawberries, sliced
> *Garnish:* sprigs of mint, dollop of yogurt

Preheat oven to 475 degrees. Combine sugar and cinnamon in a small bowl and set aside. Brush tortillas with water using a pastry brush. Sprinkle with sugar cinnamon mixture. Cut each tortilla into wedges. Spray baking sheet with nonstick cooking spray. Place wedges on baking sheet in single layer and bake 5 to 7 minutes, or until golden brown. Cool on rack or paper towels. Peel and chop apples, kiwi and orange. Put in medium-sized bowl. Place partially thawed strawberries in food processor for 20 seconds. Combine with chopped fruit and stir. Garnish as desired.

"Kids love this sweet lowfat snack.
Garnish this salsa with a sprig of mint and a dollop of yogurt, if desired."

Joan Damm   **Golden West Middle School, Fairfield, CA**

Deluxe Fajita Nachos

Serves 4

2 1/2 cups chicken, cooked, shredded
1 (1.27 ounce) package Lawry's Spices & Seasonings for Fajitas
1/3 cup water
8 ounces tortilla chips
1 1/4 cups cheddar cheese, shredded
1 cup Monterey Jack cheese, shredded
1 large tomato, chopped
1 (2.25 ounce) can ripe olives, sliced, drained
1/4 cup green onion, sliced
Garnish: salsa, guacamole, sour cream, sliced jalapeños

> **Photo Opposite**
> **Page 33**

In medium skillet, combine chicken, Spices & Seasonings for Fajitas and water; blend well. Bring to a boil; reduce heat and simmer 7 minutes. In large, shallow ovenproof platter, arrange chips. Top with chicken and cheeses. Place under broiler to melt cheese. Top with tomato, olives, green onion and desired amount of salsa. Garnish as desired. Note: 1 1/4 pounds ground beef may be substituted for chicken.

Lawry's Foods, Inc.   **www.lawrys.com**

Empañadas de Picadillo

Makes 15

1 teaspoon butter
1/2 pound lean ground beef
1/2 pound lean ground pork
1 large clove garlic, minced or pressed
1/2 cup tomato puree
1/3 cup seedless raisins
1/4 cup dry sherry
2 teaspoons ground cinnamon
1 teaspoon salt
1/2 teaspoon ground cloves
2 tablespoons vinegar
1 tablespoon sugar
3/4 cup slivered almonds
Pastry for double crust 9" pie
oil, for frying (optional)

In a wide frying pan, melt butter over medium heat. Add meat and cook, stirring often, until meat loses pinkness. Drain fat. Stir in garlic, tomato puree, raisins, sherry, cinnamon, salt, cloves, vinegar and sugar. Cook, uncovered over medium heat for 20 minutes, or until most of the liquid has evaporated. Add almonds; cool. Roll out pastry to 1/8" thickness. Cut out 3" circles for small empanadas or 4 to 5" circles for large empanadas. Spoon filling mixture evenly on one side of each pastry round; moisten edges, fold over and seal. Heat at least 1" of oil to 370 degrees. Cook until brown on both sides OR bake in a 400 degree oven for 15 to 20 minutes, until brown.

"Love these sweet 'n sour treats. From a local Mexican restaurant."

Sue Zallar   **Capistrano Valley High School, San Juan Capistrano, CA**

Empañaditos (Turnovers)

Makes 20

Filling:
1 small zucchini, cooked, diced
1 large tomato, peeled, seeded and diced
2 tablespoons green chiles, diced
3/4 cup cheddar cheese, shredded
1/8 teaspoon salt
2 teaspoons cilantro, chopped

Pastry:
2 cups flour
1 1/2 teaspoons baking powder
1 teaspoon salt
1/2 cup shortening
1/3 cup water
2 tablespoons milk
oil, for deep frying (optional)
1/4 cup milk for baking (optional)

Prepare filling by gently stirring filling ingredients together in a bowl; set aside. Pastry: Stir together flour, baking powder and salt. Cut in shortening until it resembles cornmeal. Slowly add water, stirring with fork until mixture becomes a ball. Divide dough into 20 parts. Roll each into a ball, then flatten. On a floured surface, roll each ball into a 4" circle. Place 1 tablespoon filling in center. Moisten edges with water and fold in half. Press edges with fork to seal. Either deep fry in hot oil at 375 degrees for 3 minutes OR brush with milk and bake at 425 degrees for 15 to 18 minutes until golden brown.

"Fun for a crowd. If you make them larger, they make a tasty main dish."

Priscilla Burns   **Pleasant Valley High School, Chico, CA**

Ensenada Roll-Ups

Serves 12

2 cups sour cream
2 teaspoons thyme
2 teaspoons oregano
2 teaspoons basil
2 teaspoons garlic salt or powder
2 cups cream cheese, softened
12 medium spinach leaves
24 flour tortillas
4 cups chicken, cooked, diced
3 large tomatoes, diced
1/2 cup cilantro, chopped
1 1/2 to 2 cups Monterey Jack cheese, shredded

Prepare herbed sour cream mixture by stirring into sour cream: thyme, oregano, basil and garlic salt or powder. Blend in cream cheese and mix until creamy; set aside. Wash and dry spinach leaves; cut lengthwise and set aside. Spread a small amount of herbed sour cream mixture on a flour tortilla; place spinach leaf on top followed by diced chicken and sprinkle with tomato, cilantro and cheese. Roll up, burrito-style and place in a 9" x 13" pan. Continue with remaining tortillas and filling. If desired, sprinkle cheese on top. Bake at 350 degrees for 15 to 20 minutes.

"Light and different flavors; serve with rice, beans and salsa for a complete meal. Use beef or pork instead of chicken or leave it out for a vegetarian dish."

Karen Tilson   **Poly High School, Riverside, CA**

Fiesta Rice Quesadillas

Serves 8

<table>
<tr><td>

nonstick cooking spray
1 1/2 cups water
1 1/2 cup uncooked instant white rice
1 (10 ounce) can chunk chicken, drained, shredded OR 1 1/4 cups
    cooked chicken, shredded
1 (15 ounce) jar Old El Paso Medium Cheese 'n Salsa Dip
2 (15 ounce) cans Green Giant Joan of Arc or Progresso Black Beans,
    drained, rinsed
1 (1 1/4 ounce) package Old El Paso Taco Seasoning Mix
2/3 cup water
1 cup raisins
1 (11.5 ounce) package Old El Paso Flour Tortillas
1 cup colby-Monterey Jack cheese, blend, shredded
Garnish: 1/2 to 1 cup light sour cream, 1/4 to 1 cup chopped green onions,
    1 to 3 tomatoes, chopped, 1/2 cup crushed blue tortilla chips

</td></tr>
</table>

Photo Opposite
Page 96

Preheat oven to 375 degrees. Spray large cookie sheet with nonstick cooking spray. In medium saucepan, bring 1 1/2 cups water to a boil. Stir in rice; remove from heat. Cover; let stand 5 minutes. Stir in chicken and salsa dip. Cook over medium-high heat for 2 to 3 minutes, until hot, stirring occasionally. Cover to keep warm. In another medium saucepan, combine beans, taco seasoning mix and 2/3 cup water. Bring to a boil over medium-high heat, stirring frequently. Stir in raisins. Cover to keep warm. Place 2 tortillas on cookie sheet. Spoon generous 1 cup rice mixture onto each tortilla, spreading to edges. Top each with second tortilla and 1 1/2 cups bean mixture; spreading to edges. Repeat with third tortilla and remaining rice mixture. Top each with fourth tortilla and 1/2 cup cheese, sprinkling cheese to edges of tortillas. Bake for 7 to 8 minutes or until cheese is melted and filling is hot. To serve, cut each quesadilla into 4 wedges. Garnish with sour cream, onion, tomatoes and tortilla chips.

Pillsbury Foods   **Minneapolis, MN**

Ham-Peach Empañada

Serves 8

Empanada:
2 1/2 sticks pie crust
1/2 pound ham, thinly sliced
2 fresh peaches, thinly sliced
1 cup Monterey Jack cheese, shredded

2 teaspoons dried basil
Pear Mustard:
1 fresh Bartlett pear, quartered
3 tablespoons dijon-style mustard
3 tablespoons light sour cream

Preheat oven to 450 degrees. Prepare pastry according to package directions; divide into 4 parts. On lightly floured surface, roll each into an 8" circle. Layer 1/4 of ham, peaches, cheese and basil on half of each circle. Moisten edges; fold plain half over and crimp edges to seal. Place on baking sheet and bake until golden brown, about 15 minutes. Serve hot or cold with Pear Mustard. Prepare Pear Mustard by combing pear, mustard and sour cream in blender or food processor until smooth. Refrigerate. Can be stored in an airtight container in refrigerator up to 1 week. Note: for ease in handling dough, after mixing pastry sticks and water, form into ball, wrap in waxed paper and refrigerate 30 minutes.

"Make early in the day, up to 6 hours ahead, refrigerate until ready to serve."
Nancy Schoner   **Kraemer Middle School, Placentia, CA**

Josefinas

Serves 12

1 loaf French or Italian bread or sliced bread
2 tablespoons green chiles, diced
1 stick margarine, softened
1/2 clove garlic, minced
1/2 cup mayonnaise
1/4 pound cheddar cheese, shredded

Slice loaf of bread lengthwise. If using sliced bread, toast on one side. Mix chiles, margarine and garlic until creamy; set aside. Mix mayonnaise and cheese together; set aside. Spread chile mixture on untoasted side of bread. Spread mayonnaise mixture over chiles, spreading all the way to the edges. Broil 3" from broiler until brown and puffy. Serve at once.

"From a Spanish-Cuban friend who loved to cook. I have used this recipe on many occasions... especially for Cinco de Mayo celebrations."
Phyllis Langlois   **Green Valley High School, Henderson, NV**

Macho Nachos

Serves 4

1 pound hamburger
1 onion, finely chopped
1 package taco seasoning
2/3 cup water
1 (16 ounce) can refried beans
1 (2 ounce) can green chiles, diced
2 cups jack or cheddar cheese, shredded
1 cup salsa or taco sauce
Garnish: 4 tablespoons chopped green onion, 1 cup sliced ripe olives, ripe avocado, 1 cup sour cream

In medium fry pan, crumble hamburger and add chopped onion. Fry until meat is thoroughly cooked and onion is transparent. Drain all grease from hamburger and pan. Return meat to pan; add taco seasoning and water. Simmer until mixture thickens, about 5 minutes. Place beans in an 8" x 8" pan; spread evenly. Spread hamburger mixture evenly over beans. Sprinkle chiles evenly over meat and bean mixture. Cover evenly with shredded cheese. Drizzle salsa or taco sauce over cheese. Bake, uncovered, at 400 degrees for 20 to 25 minutes or until very hot throughout. Remove from oven and garnish with green onions, olives, avocado and sour cream. Serve with tortilla chips.

"One of the students' favorites. I got this recipe out of 'Sunset' magazine in the early 70's. Always a favorite! This can also be used as a main dish."
Carol Steele   **La Paz Intermediate School, Mission Viejo, CA**

Mariachi Drumsticks

Photo Opposite
Page 32

Makes 24
1 1/4 cups tortilla chips, crushed
1 (1.0 ounce) package Lawry's Taco Spices & Seasonings
2 dozen chicken drummettes
Garnish: salsa, sour cream

In large plastic bag, combine crushed chips and Taco Spices & Seasonings. Dampen chicken with water and shake off excess. Place a few pieces at a a time in plastic bag; shake thoroughly to coat with chips. Arrange in greased shallow baking pan. Bake at 350 degrees, uncovered, 30 to 45 minutes, until crispy. Garnish as desired.
Lawry's Foods, Inc.   **www.lawrys.coms**

Mexi Cheese Sticks

Serves 8
nonstick cooking spray
1 tablespoon all purpose flour
10 ounces ready made pizza dough, unbaked
1 teaspoon chili powder
1/2 teaspoon garlic powder
1 medium jalapeño pepper, seeded, deveined and minced
1 1/2 ounces Parmesan cheese, grated
1 1/2 ounces sharp cheddar cheese, finely shredded

Preheat oven to 400 degrees. Spray baking sheet with nonstick cooking spray. Sprinkle work surface with flour. With a rolling pin, roll out pizza dough to form an 18" x 11" rectangle. Beginning at short end, sprinkle half of dough with chili and garlic powders. In small bowl, combine jalapeño with Parmesan and cheddar cheeses. Sprinkle over seasoned half of dough. Fold unseasoned half of dough over seasoned half, forming 9" x 11" rectangle; press edges together to seal. With rolling pin, roll dough several times to press filling into dough. Cut dough in half, forming 2 (4 1/2" x 11") rectangles; cut into 48 (4 1/2") strips. Twist each strip 6 or 7 times; place on prepared baking sheet, pressing ends into pan to hold in place. (If any filling escapes while twisting, sprinkle over dough. Bake 15 minutes until brown.

"A 'quick way' to make one appetizer that will take you to several parties.
It's low in fat! They freeze beautifully–just reheat and enjoy!"

Shirley Blough　　　　　　　**Hillside Junior High School, Simi Valley, CA**

Mexicali Meatballs

Makes 32

  2/3 cup A-1 Steak Sauce
  2/3 cup La Victoria Salsa
  1 1/2 pounds ground beef
  1 egg
  1/2 cup plain dry bread crumbs

Blend steak sauce and salsa in a small bowl. In a separate bowl, combine beef, egg, bread crumbs and 1/3 of the sauce mixture. Shape into 32 (1 1/4") meatballs. Place in a single layer in a shallow baking dish. Bake at 425 degrees for 15 minutes or until meat is thoroughly cooked. Drain off excess fat. Serve with remaining sauce.

"Hot and spicy!"

Pat Smith　　　　　　　**Kern Valley High School, Kern Valley, CA**

Mexican Chile-Cheese Logs

Makes 3 logs

  2 eggs
  2 slices firm-textured bread, torn into small pieces
  1 beef bouillon cube
  1 tablespoon hot water
  1/2 cup taco sauce
  2 tablespoons instant minced onion
  1 teaspoon salt
  1 1/2 teaspoons oregano leaves
  1 1/2 teaspoons chili powder
  1/2 teaspoon ground cumin
  2 2/12 cups cheddar cheese, shredded
  2 cloves garlic, minced
  1 1/4 pounds bulk pork sausage
  1 pound ground turkey
  2 (4 ounce) cans green chiles, whole
  1 (4 ounce) can black olives, sliced, drained
  3/4 teaspoon cumin seed

Beat eggs in large bowl. Add bread, bouillon, 1/4 cup taco sauce, instant minced onion, salt, oregano, chili powder, ground cumin, 1 cup cheese, garlic, sausage and turkey. Use your hands or heavy spoon to mix thoroughly. To shape logs, scoop meat onto a 12" x 20" long piece of foil. Pat meat into a neat 10" x 18" rectangle. Cut meat through foil into 3 rectangles, each 6" x 10". Split chiles and pat dry. Lay chiles flat in centers of meat rectangles; use a third of the chiles for each. Top each with 1/3 of remaining cheese, olives and cumin seed. Starting from long side, tightly roll each rectangle into a cylinder; pinch seam and ends of meat together to seal in cheese.

Peel off foil and place logs, slightly apart, on a greased 10" x 15" jelly roll pan; brush tops with remaining taco sauce. Bake in a 350 degree oven for 45 minutes or until meat feels firm when pressed. Cover; chill at least 2 hours or up to 3 days. Can also be frozen up to 2 months. To serve, slice logs into thin rounds (about 36 per log). Allow 4 to 6 thin slices per person.

"Great make-ahead appetizer. Serve with tortilla chips, small bread rounds or crisp tortilla wedges. Top with chunks of avocado or cherry tomato halves."

Sue Hope   **Lompoc High School, Lompoc, CA**

South of the Border Appetizers

Makes 12

   1 cup flour
   1/2 cup yellow cornmeal
   1/2 teaspoon chili powder
   1/4 cup butter or margarine, melted
   1/4 cup milk
   1 large egg
   1 1/2 cups sharp cheddar cheese, shredded
   1 (4 ounce) can green chiles, diced
   1/2 cup green onion, finely chopped

Mix flour, cornmeal and chili powder in a bowl. Add melted butter or margarine, milk and egg. Stir just until moistened. Press mixture evenly into a 9" square or round pan. Bake at 350 degrees approximately 20 to 25 minutes. (Corn meal mixture should be slightly browned and pull away from edge of pan.) Mix cheese, chiles and green onion together; spread over baked cornmeal. Bake additional 15 to 25 minutes, until cheese melts. Cut into wedges to serve.

"My students love this recipe. Add jalapeños if you like–to make it hotter."

Dee Moody   **Monte Vista High School, Spring Valley, CA**

Southwestern Cheesecake

Serves 10

   2 (8 ounce) packages cream cheese, softened
   16 ounces sour cream
   1 package taco seasoning mix
   3 eggs
   2 tablespoons flour
   1 (4 ounce) can green chiles, diced
   1/4 cup roasted red pepper pieces

In a food processor fitted with metal blade, combine cream cheese and sour cream; process until smooth. Add taco seasoning, eggs and flour and process until well blended. By hand, stir in chiles and red peppers. Pour into a well greased decorative copper mold. Place mold in larger baking dish which has been filled with 1" water. Bake at 350 degrees for 40 minutes to 1 hour or until sides pull away and knife inserted in center comes out dry.

"You may use two smaller molds–reduce baking time to 30 to 45 minutes."

Liz Coleman   **Oroville High School, Oroville, CA**

Sundance Pizza Stack

Makes 6

Photo Opposite
Page 97

18 (8") flour tortillas
3/4 cup corn oil
1 (24 ounce) can Angela Mia Crushed Tomatoes
3/4 cup green chiles, diced
1 (48 ounce) can Rosarita Spicy Refried Beans
3 cups Wisconsin Cheddar cheese, shredded
1 1/2 cups fresh tomatoes, chopped
2 fresh Anaheim or Poblano chiles, sliced
3/4 cup Calavo Western Style guacamole
3 green onions, chopped

Fry tortillas in oil for 10 seconds one each side until lightly browned; drain on paper towels. Combine canned tomatoes, green chiles and beans. Simmer 20 minutes, until ingredients are well blended. For each serving: spread 1/2 cup bean mixture on one tortilla. Cover with a second tortilla. Spread 1/2 cup bean mixture on second tortilla. Cover with a third tortilla. Sprinkle 1/2 cup shredded cheese, 1/4 cup fresh chopped tomatoes and 1/4 of each fresh sliced chile on third tortilla. Bake at 375 degrees for 15 minutes, until cheese melts. Remove from oven. Spoon 1 ounce guacamole on center of baked pizza. Top with 1/2 ounce chopped green onions.

Wisconsin Milk Marketing Board   **Madison, WI**

Super Nacho Casserole

Serves 10

1/2 pound chorizo
1/2 pound ground beef
1 (8 ounce) can refried beans
1 pound jack cheese, shredded
1 small can olives, sliced
1 (4 ounce) can green chiles, diced
1/2 cup sour cream
2 avocados, chopped
salsa, to taste
tortilla chips

Preheat oven to 350 degrees. In a fry pan, cook chorizo and ground beef until no longer pink; drain excess fat. In a 9" x 13" oblong pan, layer beans, meats and cheese, making two layers. Bake 15 minutes. Remove from oven and top with olives, green chiles, avocado and sour cream. Sprinkle salsa on last. Serve with tortilla chips.

"This is always a hit for Super Bowl Sunday."

Linda Silvasy   **Olive Peirce Middle School, Ramona, CA**

Taco Calzones

Serves 3 - 4

- 1/2 pound ground turkey
- 1/4 cup taco sauce
- 2 teaspoons chili powder
- 1/4 teaspoon onion powder
- 1/4 teaspoon garlic powder
- 1 package refrigerated pizza dough
- 1/4 cup Monterey Jack cheese, shredded
- 1 egg
- 1 teaspoon water

In a fry pan, cook ground turkey until browned; drain fat. Stir in taco sauce, chili powder, onion powder and garlic powder; set aside. Unroll pizza dough. Roll into a 14" x 10 1/2" rectangle. Cut into 12 squares. Divide filling among dough squares. Sprinkle with cheese. Brush edges with water. Lift one corner of each square and stretch dough to opposite corner, making a triangle. Use a fork to press edges to seal. Arrange triangles on a greased baking sheet. Prick with a fork. In a small bowl, stir together egg and water; brush onto calzones. Bake at 425 degrees for 8 to 10 minutes, until golden brown. Let stand 5 minutes before serving.

Diane Castro   **Temecula Valley High School, Temecula, CA**

Taco Cups

Serves 12

- nonstick cooking spray
- 1/2 pound ground beef
- 3 ounces water
- 1/2 package taco seasoning
- 1 tablespoon jalapeños, chopped (optional)
- 1/4 cup taco sauce (optional)
- 1 package refrigerator biscuits (regular or Hungry Jack)
- 1/4 cup cheddar cheese, shredded

Preheat oven to 350 degrees. Spray muffin pan with nonstick cooking spray. Brown meat in skillet; drain fat. Add water and taco seasoning to meat (add jalapeños or taco sauce if desired); bring to a boil. Reduce heat and cook until water is absorbed, 3 to 5 minutes. While meat is cooking, separate biscuits and roll out to fit in muffin pans. Fill each biscuit with a portion of meat and top with shredded cheese. Bake for 8 to 10 minutes or until brown. Remove and allow to cool.

"This amount is perfect for a cooking lab. The hardest part for students is rolling out the biscuits to fit the pan. You will see some funny-looking cups, but the kids will love them!"

Tricia Montelongo   **South Junior High School, Anaheim, CA**

Taquito Appetizers

Makes 30

    2 cans roast beef
    1 can corned beef
    1 teaspoon cumin
    30 corn tortillas
    1 tablespoon flour
    2 to 3 teaspoons water
    hot oil, for frying

Drain gravy from roast beef. In saucepan, heat roast beef and corned beef, breaking up with spoon. Add cumin. Warm tortillas. Place spoonful of meat in center of each tortilla and roll up tightly. Make a paste by combining flour and water. Glue ends of tortilla with paste. Heat oil on medium-high heat. Fry taquitos in hot oil and drain on paper towels. Cut into pieces and serve as appetizers.

"Everyone loves these!"

Sharon Chavez   **Rogers Middle School, Long Beach, CA**

Tortilla Chile Rolls

Makes 120

    1 package (large) flour tortillas
    4 (8 ounce) packages cream cheese, softened
    2 (4 ounce) cans green chiles, diced
    1 can ripe olives, sliced

Spread tortillas with cream cheese. Sprinkle liberally with chiles and sparingly with olives. Roll tortillas tightly and cut into 1/2" to 3/4" rolls (as you would a jelly roll).

Roberta Priestley   **Alhambra High School, Alhambra, CA**

Tortilla Roll-Ups

Serves 15 - 20

    3 (8 ounce) packages cream cheese, softened
    1 (7 ounce) can green chiles, diced
    1 (4 ounce) can black olives, chopped
    10 slices ham, thinly sliced, diced
    1 package (burrito-size) flour tortillas

Pour off any liquid from cream cheese. Combine cream cheese, chiles, olives and ham. Spread each tortilla with mixture and roll tightly. Wrap individually in plastic wrap. Refrigerate several hours or overnight. To serve, slice into 1/2" slices.

"This recipe was given to me by Jackie Gamage, a former teacher, who often prepared these for early morning staff meetings. I like the versatility of this recipe. You can add or delete items from the mixture. You can also make it lowfat by using nonfat or lowfat cream cheese. Thanks Jackie."

Maggy Flath   **Nevada Union High School, Grass Valley, CA**

Wild West Round Up

Makes 10 cups

- 1 bag Orville Redenbacher's Redenbudders Movie Theater Butter Popcorn, popped
- 1 cup Spanish peanuts
- 3 tablespoons unsalted butter
- 2 tablespoons taco seasoning mix
- 1 teaspoon chili powder
- 1/4 cup chives, chopped

Preheat oven to 350 degrees. In a large bowl, combine popcorn and peanuts. In a small saucepan, over low heat, melt butter. Add taco seasoning mix and chili powder; blend well. Dribble and toss popcorn mixture until well coated. Spread on a baking sheet. Bake for 5 minutes. Sprinkle with chopped chives.

"This snack is perfect while watching video movies at home!"

Carole Delap   **Golden West High School, Visalia, CA**

Atole

Serves 8

- 3 cups water
- 1 cup flour, sifted
- 3 cups milk
- 1 can sweetened condensed milk
- 1 tablet Grandma's Chocolate dissolved in 1 cup water
- sugar, to taste

Boil 2 cups water. Mix together 1 cup flour and remaining 1 cup water. Pour through a strainer into boiling water, stirring constantly. After water and flour become thick, add milk. Heat until boiling, stirring constantly. Add condensed milk and chocolate. Stir well, adding sugar to taste.

"Students love making this traditional drink at Christmas time."

Charlotte Runyan   **Saddleback High School, Santa Ana, CA**

Cherimoya Tropical Smoothie

Serves 2

- 1 ripe cherimoya, pulped and seeded
- 1 cup Thrifty brand Apricot Mango Sherbet
- 1 banana, cut up
- 3 strawberries, frozen
- 2 cups orange juice

Place all ingredients into a blender and mix to a slushy consistency. Add more orange juice, if desired.

"Cherimoya fruit is becoming more available. Purchase hard and allow to ripen at room temperature 2 to 4 days before refrigerating. Skin may darken but the pulp is not affected. The fruit has a silky-smooth cream colored pulp."

Gloria Francuch   **Carpinteria High School, Carpinteria, CA**

Chocolate Mexicano

Serves 8

2 quarts + 1/2 cup milk, divided
2 (2") sticks cinnamon
1/2 cup cocoa
1 cup sugar
1/4 cup cornmeal
1 teaspoon vanilla

In saucepan, heat 2 quarts milk with cinnamon sticks until almost boiling. In a bowl, stir cocoa, sugar, cornmeal and vanilla into 1/2 cup milk, stirring until thick sauce forms. Remove cinnamon sticks and pour sauce into heated milk, stirring constantly with beater. Lower heat and serve at once.

"One of our Spanish teachers shared this recipe. A favorite of the Spanish Club."
Judith Huffman   **Mariposa County High School, Mariposa, CA**

Mexican Coffee

Serves 4

5 - 7 cinnamon sticks, about 3" long
1/2 cup ground coffee, regular or decaffeinated
1 cone piloncilla, about 3 ounces, chopped OR 1/4 cup brown sugar
4 cups water

Break one cinnamon stick in half. Place ground coffee in filter of drip-style coffeemaker. Scatter broken cinnamon stick and piloncilla over coffee. Brew coffee with 4 cups water. Pour into 4 six ounce cups; garnish each cup with cinnamon stick.

"This recipe is from Sunset's Low-Fat Mexican Cookbook. It's a satisfying way to end a meal and only 46 calories per serving."
Myrna Swearingen   **Corona High School, Corona, CA**

Mexican Fruit Punch

Makes 2 quarts

1 cup sugar
1 1/2 cups water
4 sticks cinnamon
12 cloves
1 (46 ounce) can pineapple juice
1 1/2 cups orange juice
1/2 cup lemon juice
1 quart ginger ale (optional)

Simmer sugar, water, cinnamon and cloves for 30 minutes; strain, removing cinnamon and cloves. Add pineapple, orange and lemon juices. Pour over ice or frozen pineapple juice cubes. Add ginger ale for a sparkling punch.

"Freeze cherry halves or mint in ice cubes for additional color and flavor."
Janet Policy   **Ramona High School, Riverside, CA**

Mock Margarita Punch

Serves 12

    1 (6 ounce) can frozen lemonade concentrate
    1 (6 ounce) can frozen limeade concentrate
    $1/4$ cup powdered sugar
    3 cups crushed ice
    2 cups club soda, chilled
    lime wedges
    coarse salt

In blender, combine concentrates, powdered sugar and ice. Cover and blend until slushy. Add club soda and gently stir. If desired, rub rim of each glass with lime slice and dip in coarse salt. Fill each glass with slush mixture.

"A refreshing non-alcoholic punch!"

Shirley Marshman   **West Middle School, Downey, CA**

Nancy's Hot Poppers

Serves 6

    12 to 20 small light green chile peppers
    1 (8 ounce) package cream cheese, softened
    2 eggs, well beaten
    1 tablespoon flour
    1 to 2 cups corn flake crumbs
    2 tablespoons taco seasoning
    oil for deep fat frying

Split chiles half way to remove seeds. Fill with cream cheese. Close chile and freeze for approximately 2 hours. Prepare a batter by beating eggs with flour. In a pie plate or flat dish, stir together corn flake crumbs and taco seasoning. Heat oil for deep frying. Dip chiles in batter and roll in corn flake mixture. Fry approximately 3 minutes, until golden brown.

"This recipe is very good. Any hot chile may be used,
but my family prefers mild chiles grown in the garden."

Nancy Albers   **Lassen High School, Susanville, CA**

Shrimp Stuffed Avocados

Serves 4

2 tablespoons vinegar
1 1/2 teaspoons lemon juice
1/4 teaspoon salt
1/8 teaspoon dry mustard
dash pepper
12 ounces (medium) shrimp, fresh or frozen, shelled and deveined
1 small onion, thinly sliced
1 clove garlic, halved
3 tablespoons oil
1 small pickled jalapeño pepper, cut in strips
2 avocados, halved and seeded
1 medium tomato, chopped

In a bowl, combine vinegar, lemon juice, salt, mustard and pepper; set aside. In medium skillet, cook shrimp, half the onion slices and garlic in hot oil over medium-high heat 4 to 5 minutes or until shrimp are done, stirring occasionally. Remove onion and garlic with slotted spoon and discard. Add shrimp and remaining oil to vinegar mixture in bowl along with remaining onion and jalapeño. Cover and chill several hours or overnight, stirring occasionally. To serve, spoon into avocado halves. Sprinkle with chopped tomato and drizzle marinade over.

"I love to serve this as an appetizer when I have guests or as a main dish in summer. A great way to use those wonderful local avocados! I add cilantro to it!"
Sheryl Malone   **Mt. Carmel High School, San Diego, CA**

SALSAS & DIPS

7-Layer Mexican Dip

Serves 8

- 1 (8 ounce) package cream cheese, softened
- 1 tablespoon taco seasoning mix
- 1 cup prepared guacamole
- 1 cup salsa
- 1 cup lettuce, shredded
- 1 cup cheddar cheese, shredded
- $1/2$ cup green onion, chopped
- 2 tablespoons ripe olives, sliced
- tortilla chips

Blend together cream cheese and taco seasoning mix. Spread on bottom of 9" pie plate. Layer remaining ingredients over cream cheese. Refrigerate at least 1 hour. Serve with tortilla chips.

"You can adjust the spiciness of the dip depending on salsa used. You may add diced jalapeño peppers, if desired."

Sally Engel   **Elsinore Middle School, Lake Elsinore, CA**

Avocado Dip

Serves 8

6 to 8 avocados
1 medium onion, finely chopped
1 to 2 tomatoes, chopped
1/2 head lettuce, shredded
1 (7 ounce) can green chile salsa
1/4 teaspoon garlic salt
1/2 cup cheddar cheese, shredded

Peel and mash avocados. Add remaining ingredients except cheese. Mix well. Top with cheese and serve with chips. Note: Keep seeds in dip to prevent browning.

"A little different twist on traditional guacamole."

Trena Becker   **Ball Junior High School, Anaheim, CA**

Blender Salsa

Makes 2 cups

3 medium tomatoes, chopped
8 jalapeño chiles, chopped
1 clove garlic, chopped
1/4 cup onion, chopped
1 bunch cilantro, chopped
1/2 teaspoon salt
1/4 cup water

In a small pan, simmer tomatoes and chiles for 10 minutes; drain. Place in blender and add remaining ingredients. Blend until smooth.

*"This recipe was shared with me by Juan Abea, Nicolasa Damian
and Norma Lopez, students in my Single Survival Class."*

Vanessa VanAssen   **Fort Bragg High School, Fort Bragg, CA**

Chorizo Chili Cheese Dip

Serves 8 - 10

10 ounces chorizo sausage
1 can chili, no beans
1 (16 ounce) bag Fritos or tortilla chips
1 pound cheese, shredded

Heat oven to 300 degrees. Cook chorizo sausage in skillet; add chili and heat through. In a 9" x 13" pan, layer 1/2 the chips, 1/2 chili mixture and 1/2 cheese. Repeat. Bake for 15 minutes, or until cheese melts.

*"I got this recipe from one of my student's mom.
We made it in my Home Ec class and it was a big hit."*

Cindy Bowman   **McFarland High School, McFarland, CA**

Creamy Guacamole

Serves 6

3 avocados, fully ripened
juice from 1/2 lemon
salt, to taste
1/4 cup sour cream
3 to 4 dashes Tabasco sauce
1/2 onion, diced (optional)
1 tomato, diced (optional)

Peel and mash avocados with potato masher. Add lemon juice, salt, sour cream and Tabasco sauce. Taste; adjust seasonings. Tomato and onion may be added, if desired.

Nancy Hunyadi **Fullerton High School, Fullerton, CA**

Eloise's Special Chili Dip

Serves 8

8 ounces Velveeta cheese, cubed
1 can chili, no beans
1 (4 ounce) can green chiles, diced
corn chips, for dipping

Heat cheese, chili and green chiles together over medium heat, stirring occasionally, until cheese is melted. Serve with chips.

Eloise Hatfield **Poston Junior High School, Mesa, AZ**

Fresh & Chunky Salsa

Makes 2 - 3 cups

1 1/2 tomatoes, chopped
2 tablespoons green chiles, diced
1 green onion, diced
1/4 green pepper, diced
1 tablespoon lemon juice
2 tablespoons cilantro, chopped
1 clove garlic, minced
1/4 cup tomato sauce
pinch pepper

Combine all ingredients except tomato sauce. In a blender, puree 1/2 cup salsa mixture with tomato sauce. Add puree to salsa mixture, stir and chill before serving (overnight is best).

*"My students make this recipe with homemade chips every year.
They love it! Hot sauce can be added to make it hot!"*

Laury White **Fallbrook High School, Fallbrook, CA**
Nancy Tollefson **Poston Junior High School, Mesa, AZ**

Fresh Guacamole with Homemade Chips

Serves 6

2 ripe avocados
juice from 1 lemon
2 tablespoons chile sauce or salsa
6 corn tortillas

Preheat oven to 400 degrees. Peel and mash avocados. Add lemon juice and salsa and mix well; refrigerate. Lay tortillas directly onto oven rack and bake 5 minutes; turn with tongs and bake 5 minutes more until desired brownness. Remove, break into chips and use with dip.

"These chips are lowfat and very toasty tasting."

Jane Souza   **No. Monterey Co. High School, Castroville, CA**

Fresh Peach Salsa

Makes 2 cups

2 cups fresh peaches, peeled, chopped
1/4 cup sweet onion, chopped
3 tablespoons lime juice
2 to 3 tablespoons fresh jalapeño pepper, seeded, finely chopped
1 clove garlic, minced
1 tablespoon cilantro, chopped
1/2 teaspoon sugar

In a medium mixing bowl, gently stir together all ingredients. Cover and chill 1 to 2 hours.

"Great served with tortilla chips or spooned over grilled pork, chicken or fish."

Julie Shelburne   **Tulare Union High School, Tulare, CA**

Fruit & Vegetable Salsa

Makes 1 quart

1 cucumber, peeled and diced
1 large or 2 small peaches, peeled and diced
1 small onion, diced
1 bottle mild salsa

In large bowl, combine cucumber, peaches and onion. Pour salsa over top and gently toss. Serve.

"Be sure to use MILD salsa as it is already spicy."

Sherrie Miles   **Cimarron-Memorial High School, Las Vegas, NV**

Gazpacho Dip

Serves 4

4 to 5 green onions, sliced
1 (4 ounce) can ripe olives, chopped
1 (4 ounce) can green chiles, diced
1 (8 ounce) can tomato sauce
1 (16 ounce) can whole tomatoes, chopped
4 tablespoons olive oil
3 tablespoons wine vinegar
salt, garlic salt and Tabasco sauce, to taste
corn chips

Combine all ingredients. Chill at least 2 hours or overnight. Serve with corn chips.

Connie Sweet   **Rim Of The World High School, Lake Arrowhead, CA**

Green Chile and Cheese Dip

Makes 2 1/2 cups

1 medium onion, chopped
2 tablespoons salad oil
1 (4 ounce) can green chiles, diced
1-1/2 tablespoons flour
1/4 cup chicken broth
1/2 cup sour cream
1 can pimentos, chopped
3 cups mild cheddar or longhorn cheese, shredded
tortilla chips

In a frying pan, saute onion in oil until translucent. Add chiles and cook another minute. Blend in flour. Gradually add broth, then sour cream. Heat until just boiling and slightly thickened. Reduce heat and add pimentos. Gradually stir in shredded cheese, stirring until melted. To serve, keep dip warm using a chafing dish or warming tray; scoop on to tortilla chips to eat.

"Can turn out moderate to hot, depending on the chiles. Add 1 or 2 ounces diced jalapeños for zest! Add a layer of this sauce to the 7-Layer Mexican dip!"

Colleen Easton   **Brea-Olinda High School, Brea, CA**

Guacamole With Chiles and Cilantro

Makes 2 cups

2 medium avocados, peeled
1 tablespoon lime or lemon juice
1 small tomato, peeled, finely chopped
2 tablespoons onion, finely chopped
2 tablespoons green chiles, diced
1 clove garlic, minced
1/2 teaspoon cilantro, finely chopped (optional)
1/4 teaspoon salt

Mash avocado with fork or potato masher; add lime or lemon juice and mix well. Stir in tomato, onions, chiles, garlic, cilantro and salt; mix well. Serve as a dip with with corn chips or as a sauce with main dishes.

"Authentic guacamole has a coarse, chunky texture.
Purists say the flavors are milder when mashed by hand than when pureed.
To prevent the mixture from discoloring, cover the guacamole during storage."

Deanna Lee   **Marina High School, Huntington Beach, CA**

Helen's Three-Alarm Salsa

Makes 2 cups

> 5 yellow chiles
> 1 jalapeño pepper
> 1 serrano chile
> 1 (16 ounce) can whole tomatoes, cut into small pieces
> 1/2 medium onion
> 5 cloves garlic
> 1 bunch fresh cilantro
> 1/2 teaspoon oregano
> 1/2 teaspoon cumin powder
> salt and pepper, to taste

Roast chiles on a cast iron tortilla warmer or in the oven. After roasting, chop off stems. (Remove all seeds for a milder sauce.) Drain tomatoes, reserving juice; chop tomatoes and set aside. In a blender, chop onion, garlic, chiles and spices in the juice from the can of tomatoes. After blending, stir in tomatoes and chopped cilantro.

"I borrowed this recipe from Gloria Karimi from Azusa High School.
It is a traditional family recipe, named after her mother.
'Gringos' may wish to eliminate the serrano and some of the jalapeño chiles."

Linda Winzenread   **Whittier High School, Whittier, CA**

Jalapeño Special

Makes 1 quart

> 8 to 10 Roma tomatoes, finely chopped
> 2 to 3 jalapeño chiles, with seeds
> 1 cup onion, chopped
> 2 to 3 cloves garlic, minced
> 1/4 cup fresh cilantro, chopped
> 2 to 3 assorted chiles: green, serrano or yellow, finely chopped
> 1/2 teaspoon garlic salt
> 1/4 teaspoon black pepper

Lightly toss vegetables and chiles together with garlic salt and black pepper. Serve with tacos, as a condiment or serve with tortilla chips.

"Spread it on tortilla chips and sprinkle with grated cheese, then bake as Nachos.
Be sure to serve with plenty of water as it is a bit spicy."

Debra Jamison   **Basic High School, Henderson, NV**

Killer Tostada Dip

Serves 6 - 8

      2 cans bean dip
      3 avocados, peeled, seeded, diced
      lemon juice
      garlic salt and pepper, to taste
      1 cup sour cream
      1 cup mayonnaise
      1 package Lawry's Taco Seasoning
      2 (small) cans olives, sliced
      2 bunches green onions, sliced
      3 medium tomatoes, chopped
      2 to 3 cups cheddar cheese, shredded
      tortilla chips

Spread bean dip on serving platter. In a bowl, mix avocado, lemon juice, garlic salt and pepper together and spread over bean dip. Mix together sour cream, mayonnaise and taco seasoning; spread over avocado. Sprinkle with olives, green onions, tomatoes and cheddar cheese. Serve with tortilla chips.

"A great recipe for the Super Bowl!"

Brenda Umbro   **Orange Glen High School, Escondido, CA**

Lowfat Layered Bean Dip

Serves 18

      1 (15 ounce) can red kidney beans, drained
      1/4 cup salsa
      1 (4 ounce) can green chiles, diced
      1/2 cup roasted red pepper, drained and chopped
      1 cup lowfat cottage cheese
      1 cup tomato, chopped
      1/4 cup lowfat cheddar cheese, shredded
      Tortilla chips

In a blender, place beans and salsa. Cover and blend until smooth. Spread mixture evenly in a 9" pie plate. Sprinkle with green chiles and roasted red pepper. Wash blender. Place cottage cheese in blender and process until smooth. Spread cottage cheese on top of bean mixture. Cover and chill at least 4 hours. Before serving, sprinkle with tomato and cheddar cheese. Serve with tortilla chips.

"Taken from Better Homes & Gardens New Dieter's Cookbook.
It's low fat, low cholesterol and very tasty!"

Melissa Webb   **Lakewood High School, Lakewood, CA**

Mexican Chile Dip

Serves 10

      2 bunches green onions, chopped
      2 cans green chiles, chopped

Mariachi Drumsticks
Spice up an old favorite!
Page 16

Deluxe Fajita Nachos
Made with
shredded chicken!
Page 12

2 (small) cans black olives, chopped
2 ripe tomatoes, finely chopped
1 jar pimentos, chopped (optional)
6 tablespoons wine vinegar
3 tablespoons olive or vegetable oil
salt, to taste
pepper, to taste
garlic salt, to taste
seasoned salt, to taste

Mix all ingredients together. Season to your liking with salt and pepper, garlic salt and seasoned salt. Serve with crackers or chips.

"A different, fresh tasting dip."

Sandra Robertson   **Whittier High School, Whittier, CA**

Mexican Jumping Bean Dip

Serves 6

8 ounces cream cheese, softened
1 can chili, no meat
1/4 cup hot salsa
dash Tabasco sauce
flour tortillas

Preheat oven to 350 degrees. In a saucepan, over medium-high heat, melt cream cheese with chili; do not boil. Stirring constantly, add salsa and Tabasco sauce. When thoroughly combined, remove from heat. In oven, heat tortillas on oven rack at 350 degrees for 10 to 15 minutes until crispy. Cut tortillas into wedges and use them to dip.

"This is a quick and easy dip that everyone loves."

Alicia Pucci   **Kenilworth Junior High School, Petaluma, CA**

Nonfat Black Bean and Corn Salsa

Makes 3 quarts

1 can Mexican stewed tomatoes
1 medium fresh tomato, diced
1/2 bunch cilantro, finely chopped
1 bunch green onions, finely chopped
1 medium purple onion, finely chopped
2 (15 ounce) cans black beans
2 (15 ounce) cans corn
pinch garlic salt
pinch pepper
pinch cumin
pinch red pepper

Mix all ingredients and marinate overnight. Taste next day and adjust seasonings.

"Serve with meat or chips of your choice."

Connie Willems   **Paulding Middle School, Arroyo Grande, CA**

Paul's Fiesta Bean Dip

Serves 4

> 1 can refried beans
> 1/4 cup onion, finely diced
> 1 tomato, diced
> 1 (small) can olives, sliced
> 1/2 avocado, diced
> 1/2 cup mild taco sauce
> 1/2 cup cheddar cheese, shredded

Spread beans evenly in a 9" pie pan. Sprinkle with onion, tomato, olives and avocado. Spread taco sauce evenly over top, then sprinkle with shredded cheese. Bake at 300 degrees for 10 to 15 minutes, just until cheese is slightly melted.

Ann Porter   **San Luis Obispo High School, San Luis Obispo, CA**

Picante Black Bean Pizza Dip

Serves 8

> 2 (15 ounce) cans black beans, rinsed, drained
> 1 cup Pace Picante Sauce
> 1 (3 ounce) package cream cheese, softened
> 3 cloves garlic, minced
> 2 teaspoons ground cumin
> 1 teaspoon dried oregano
> 1 teaspoon dried basil
> 1/2 cup pepperoni, finely chopped
> 1 cup mozzarella cheese, shredded
> 1/2 cup red and green bell pepper, chopped
> 1/4 cup ripe olive slices
> tortilla chips or vegetable dippers, for dipping

In food processor, fitted with steel blade, process beans until fairly smooth; transfer to mixing bowl (or mash beans with a potato masher). Add 1/2 cup picante sauce, cream cheese, garlic and seasonings; mix well. Spread evenly into 9" pie plate. Top evenly with remaining picante sauce. Sprinkle with pepperoni. Bake at 350 degrees for 20 minutes or until hot. Sprinkle evenly with mozzarella cheese, garnish with peppers and olives. Serve warm with chips or vegetable dippers.

Betty Rabin   **Sierra Vista Junior High School, Canyon Country, CA**

Spicy Baked Dip

Serves 10

> 1 (1 pound 14 ounce) can refried beans
> 3 tablespoons jalapeño pepper, chopped
> 1 pound ground beef
> 1 pound jack cheese, shredded
> 2 to 3 green onions, chopped
> 1 medium bell pepper, chopped
> 1 (4.5 ounce) can olives, chopped

1 avocado, chopped
2 small tomatoes, chopped
Tortilla chips

Mix beans with jalapeños. Spread on large pizza pan. Cook ground beef; drain. Spread beef on top of beans and sprinkle with cheese, onions, bell pepper and olives. Bake at 350 degrees for 15 to 20 minutes. Sprinkle with avocado and tomatoes. Serve with tortilla chips.

"My sister gave me this recipe. She's a great sister and this is a great appetizer!"
Cheryl McDaniels **Green Valley High School, Henderson, NV**

Tex-Mex Caviar Dip

Serves 25

3 (16 ounce) cans black-eyed peas
1 (7 ounce) can green chiles, diced
1 small jar pimento, diced
1 (8 ounce) bottle Wishbone Italian dressing
1 (8 ounce) jar Picante sauce
1 onion, diced
1 bell pepper, diced
Corn chips

Mash peas and mix with other ingredients. Place in shallow baking dish. Bake at 350 degrees for 20 minutes. Cool to set. Serve with corn chips.

"Delicious while watching those football games!"
Sonja Tyree **Ayala High School, Chino, CA**

Tomato Corn Salsa

Serves 4

1 fresh hot green chile pepper
1 1/2 pounds fresh tomatoes, seeded and chopped
1 1/2 cups frozen corn, thawed
3 green onions, thinly sliced
1 tablespoon fresh parsley, chopped
1 tablespoon fresh cilantro, chopped
2 tablespoons fresh lemon or lime juice
2 tablespoons olive oil
1 teaspoon salt

Roast the chile over a flame, using tongs, charring all sides until blistered. Place in plastic bag and let rest about 5 minutes. Rub off charred skin (discard seeds if milder salsa is desired). Chop chile into small pieces and place in bowl. Add remaining ingredients and gently toss to blend. Cover with plastic wrap and refrigerate until ready to serve.

Note: Use plastic gloves to rub off charred skin from chile. This will eliminate getting any hot chile juice on the skin and possibly the eyes–which can be very painful.

"Serve with barbecued meats or in burritos."
Linda Falkenstien **Morro Bay High School, Morro Bay, CA**

Albondigas Soup

Serves 8

Meatballs:
1/2 pound ground beef
1/2 pound ground pork
1/2 cup bread crumbs
1 egg
2 tablespoons milk
1 teaspoon salt
1/2 teaspoon oregano
1/2 teaspoon cumin
1/4 cup onion, minced
Broth:
5 (10.5 ounce) cans beef bouillon
1 quart water
1 (28 ounce) can tomatoes, chopped
1/2 cup salsa
1/2 teaspoon basil
1/2 teaspoon oregano
salt and pepper, to taste
Optional: potato, celery, carrot, cilantro

Prepare meatballs by mixing ingredients with hands in a bowl; form into balls. Combine broth ingredients in large saucepan and bring to a boil. Add meatballs, cover and cook on low heat for 40 minutes.

"I always add the optional ingredients for more flavor and nutrition."

Janet Riness   **Westminster High School, Westminster, CA**

Chicken Soup Olé

Serves 8

4 boneless skinless chicken breast halves, all fat removed
4 cups water
2 (14.5 ounce) cans stewed tomatoes, undrained
2 teaspoons chicken flavor bouillon
1 (4 ounce) can green chiles, diced
1 teaspoon chili powder
$1/2$ teaspoon ground cumin
$1/4$ teaspoon garlic powder
$1/4$ teaspoon ground red pepper
1 cup frozen whole kernel corn
$1/2$ cup zucchini, chopped

In large saucepan over medium-high heat, combine all ingredients except corn and zucchini; bring to a boil. Reduce heat to low; cover and simmer 30 minutes. Remove chicken, cut into cubes. Return chicken to pan, add corn and zucchini; simmer 10 minutes more. Serve.

Jennifer Walker   **Bloomington High School, Bloomington, CA**

Crock Pot Green Chili Soup

Serves 8

2 tablespoons oil
2 pounds stew meat or pork, or round steak, cubed
1 onion, chopped
2 cloves garlic, minced
1 green bell pepper, chopped
1 teaspoon cumin
salt and pepper, to taste
2 (14.5 ounce) cans beef broth
4 medium potatoes, diced
2 (7 ounce) cans green chiles, diced
1 cup water
Garnish: flour tortillas or tortilla chips, shredded cheese

Heat oil in skillet. Add meat, onion, garlic and green pepper; brown. Place in crock pot. Add cumin, salt, pepper, beef broth, potatoes, canned chiles and water. Cook all day, until meat is tender. Serve in bowls with garnishes.

Note: If you would like to make this soupier, add a cup of water and a bouillon cube as many times as needed to get the consistency you desire.

"You can also make this in a Dutch oven. Cook on low to medium heat for 1 hour."

Lura Staffanson   **Centennial High School, Corona, CA**

Easy Tortilla Soup

Serves 8

    2 cloves garlic, minced
    1 tablespoon oil
    1 (49.5 ounce) can chicken broth
    2 (10.5 ounce) cans French Onion soup
    1 (14.5 ounce) can Mexcian-Style stewed tomatoes, chopped
    1 (5.5 ounce) can V-8 Juice
    6 to 8 corn tortillas, cut into strips
    1 1/2 cups jack cheese, shredded
    Garnish: fresh chopped cilantro, diced avocado

In a large pot, slowly saute garlic in oil. Add chicken broth, French onion soup, tomatoes and V-8 juice. Cover and bring to a boil. Lower heat and simmer 15 to 30 minutes. Fry or bake tortilla strips at 350 degrees for 15 to 20 minutes until crisp. To serve, put tortilla strips in bowls, ladle in soup, then top with generous helping of cheese on top. Garnish as desired.

"Easy and delicious."

Susan Lefler　　　　　　　　　　　**Ramona Junior High School, Chino, CA**

El Torito's Sopa De Tortilla

Serves 12

    2 chicken breast halves, boneless, skinless
    3 quarts chicken broth
    1 red onion, diced
    2 carrots, diced
    1 potato, diced
    1/4 cup tomato paste
    1 bay leaf
    2 cloves garlic, chopped
    1/2 teaspoon Chipotle chile en adobo, pureed
    1 teaspoon pickled jalapeño chile, seeded, chopped
    1 teaspoon dried Mexican oregano
    1/8 teaspoon ground cumin
    salt and pepper, to taste
    1 zucchini, diced
    1 yellow hookneck squash, diced
    1/2 red bell pepper, diced
    juice of 1 lime
    2 tablespoons sweet sherry
    1 tablespoon cilantro, chopped
    1 tablespoon fresh mint
    4 corn tortillas, cut into thin strips
    oil, for frying
    1/2 pound jack cheese, shredded
    12 slices avocado
    cilantro springs, for garnish

Poach chicken in simmering broth until cooked through, approximately 10 minutes. Set aside to cool enough to shred. Combine broth, shredded chicken, red onion, carrots, potato, tomato paste, bay leaf, garlic, chiles, oregano, cumin and salt and pepper, to taste. Bring to a boil, then reduce heat to simmer; simmer 20 minutes. Add zucchini, hookneck, bell pepper, lime juice and sherry. Bring to a boil again; reduce heat and simmer 15 minutes. Add chopped cilantro and mint. Stir, then remove from heat. Fry tortilla strips in hot oil until crisp. Drain on paper towels and set aside. Ladle soup into each bowl. Sprinkle with shredded cheese and tortilla strips. Garnish each bowl with avocado slices and sprigs of cilantro. Serve immediately.

Note: Soup may be frozen, if desired.

"Don't be put off by the long ingredient list. This is an outstanding, spicy soup!"

Sally Reimers   **Valley View Middle School, Simi Valley, CA**

Fiesta Corn Chowder

Serves 6 - 8

- 1/2 cup carrots, finely chopped
- 1/2 cup celery, finely chopped
- 1 can chicken broth
- 2 (15 ounce) cans creamed corn OR 1 can creamed, 1 can whole kernel corn
- 2 cups ham, turkey or chicken, finely diced
- 1 teaspoon to 1 tablespoon jalapeño chiles, diced
- salt and pepper, to taste
- 1/2 cup milk or half & half
- bacon bits, for garnish

In a large saucepan, cook carrots and celery in chicken broth until tender. Add corn, ham, jalapeños, salt, pepper and milk or half and half. Simmer 30 to 40 minutes, stirring frequently to avoid sticking. Garnish with bacon bits. Serve piping hot.

"Flavor will be enhanced if prepared and refrigerated 24 hours before serving."

Mary Lash   **Paramount High School, Paramount, CA**

Green Chile Chicken Soup

Serves 5

- 2 poblano chiles
- 2 teaspoons vegetable oil
- 1 onion, chopped
- 1 red bell pepper, seeded, chopped
- 1 carrot, chopped
- 3 cloves garlic, chopped
- 5 cups chicken broth
- 1 small can tomatoes
- 1 tablespoon fresh basil, or 1 teaspoon dried basil
- 1 cup cooked chicken, shredded
- 1 can whole kernel corn

Roast poblano chile over direct flame; place in a paper bag for 20 minutes, to steam. Remove from bag, peel and chop. Heat oil in a large pan. Add onion, bell pepper, carrots and garlic; saute until soft. Add broth, tomatoes, basil, chicken and corn. Bring to a boil, then lower heat and simmer 30 minutes. Serve hot.

Toni Purtill   **Basic High School, Henderson, NV**

Joanne's Posole

Serves 8

    1 teaspoon olive oil
    1 pound pork tenderloin, chopped
    4 boneless chicken breast halves, chopped
    3 to 4 yellow or green chiles, seeded, chopped
    1 teaspoon garlic, chopped
    1 onion, chopped
    1 bunch cilantro, chopped
    1/4 bunch parsley, chopped
    4 carrots, diced
    1 (29 ounce) can hominy, including liquid
    3 (16 ounce) cans chicken broth
    2 red chiles, dried
    2 bay leaves
    1 teaspoon oregano
    1/2 cup white wine
    2 tablespoons cornstarch, optional

In a large skillet or stock pot, brown pork and chicken in olive oil. In another skillet, quickly saute chiles, garlic, onion, cilantro and parsley; add to browned meat. Immediately add chicken broth and remaining ingredients, except cornstarch. Bring slowly to just below boiling. Reduce heat and simmer 1 to 1 1/2 hours. Just before serving, blend in cornstarch to thicken liquid, if desired.

Note: Peppers are hot! Adjust amount used according to desired hotness!

Joanne Vogel   **Marina High School, Huntington Beach, CA**

Lowfat Mexican Cheese Soup

Serves 4

    nonstick cooking spray
    1/2 cup onion, finely chopped
    1/2 cup celery, finely chopped
    3 tablespoons green pepper, finely chopped
    1 (14.5 ounce) can reduced sodium chicken broth
    3/4 cup reduced fat sharp cheddar cheese, shredded
    1 tablespoon corn starch
    1/2 cup nonfat milk
    1 (12 ounce) can evaporated skim milk
    1/3 cup mild salsa
    2 tablespoons nonfat plain yogurt
    9 to 10 drops hot pepper sauce
    1 tablespoon chives, chopped
    tortilla chips (optional)

Lightly coat an unheated large skillet with nonstick cooking spray. Add onions, celery, green peppers and 2 tablespoons broth. Cook and stir over medium heat about 8 minutes or until celery is tender. (If necessary, add more chicken broth.) Add remaining broth, bring to a simmer. Meanwhile place cheddar cheese in small bowl and sprinkle with cornstarch; toss until coated. Slowly stir cheese into broth mixture. Cook and stir over low heat just until cheese is melted. Stir in nonfat milk, evaporated skim milk, salsa, yogurt and hot pepper sauce. Heat just until warm, stirring occasionally. Ladle soup into small soup bowls and top with chives. Serve with tortilla chips.

"Per serving: 163 calories; 3.8 grams fat, 13 mg. cholesterol."

Kathie Baczynski   **Mt. Carmel High School, Poway, CA**

Mexican Posole

Serves 18

    3 pounds lean pork, with bone
    3 large onions, chopped
    6 to 8 cups tomatoes. chopped
    2 (28 ounce) cans hominy
    1/4 to 1/2 cup green chiles, diced
    12 cups water (approximate)
    Garnish: 1 head shredded lettuce, lime wedges

Brown meat on all sides in large skillet. Add onions; saute until golden brown. Add tomatoes, hominy and green chiles; mix gently. Cover with water. Cook, covered over low heat for 3 hours, stirring occasionally. Cool. Refrigerate if possible. Skim fat from soup and discard. Remove meat and shred or cut into bite sized pieces. Return to soup and reheat. To serve, top with shredded lettuce and pass lime wedges to squeeze on top.

"My friends, who are from Mexico, do not use the tomatoes, but it is so good this way. It may be cooked, uncovered, for 30 minutes longer, to reduce liquid."

Carole Call   **Costa Mesa High School, Costa Mesa, CA**

Pam's Gazpacho

Serves 4

    3 cups tomato juice
    3/4 cup celery, chopped
    3/4 cup cucumber, chopped
    1/2 cup onion, chopped
    1/4 cup green pepper, chopped
    1 tablespoon dried parsley or 2 tablespoons fresh parsley, minced
    3 tablespoons wine vinegar
    2 tablespoons olive oil
    1 teaspoon salt
    1/4 teaspoon pepper
    1/2 teaspoon worcestershire sauce
    dash garlic powder

Using a glass or stainless steel bowl, combine all ingredients; cover and refrigerate overnight. Serve chilled.

"This is so easy, healthy and delicious!
Many thanks to my friend Pam, for sharing this recipe with me!"

Jan Schulenburg   **Irvine High School, Irvine, CA**

Picante Black Bean & Rice Soup

Serves 6

    1 medium onion, chopped
    1/2 cup celery, diced
    2 cloves garlic, minced
    2 tablespoons margarine
    2 (14 ounce) cans chicken broth
    1 medium red bell pepper, diced
    1/2 teaspoon oregano, crushed
    1/2 teaspoon lemon peel, finely shredded
    1 bay leaf
    2 (16 ounce) cans black beans, undrained
    1 cup instant rice
    3/4 cup Pace Picante sauce

In a large saucepan, cook onion, celery and garlic in margarine until tender, about 4 minutes. Stir in broth, red pepper, oregano, lemon peel and bay leaf. Bring to a boil; reduce heat and simmer, uncovered 5 minutes. Stir in beans, rice and picante sauce. Return to boil. Cover and let stand 5 minutes. Discard bay leaf. Ladle into soup bowls; serve with additional picante sauce.

Pat Curtis   **Ensign Intermediate School, Newport Beach, CA**

Pine Nut Soup

Serves 4 - 6

    1 pound raw pinon nuts (pine nuts)
    2 green onions, with tops, chopped
    2 coriander seeds
    1 teaspoon dried mint, crushed
    1/2 teaspoon salt
    1/4 teaspoon pepper
    1 quart milk
    1 cup water
    2 cups chicken broth
    Garnish: crumbled corn chips

Combine all ingredients (except crumbled corn chips) in large soup pot; simmer, stirring frequently for 1/2 hour. Remove from heat and mash or puree in blender. Reheat or serve cold with crumbled corn chips.

"Interesting flavor for a change."

Stephanie San Sebastian   **Central High School, Fresno, CA**

Sopa de Fideo

Serves 4

    2 tablespoons olive oil
    1 package coiled fideo pasta
    1/2 onion, chopped
    2 cloves garlic, minced
    1 (16 ounce) can tomato sauce
    4 cups water
    2 bouillon cubes, chicken, beef or vegetarian

In large skillet, heat olive oil over medium-high heat. Fry fideo pasta with onion and garlic until slightly browned; do not burn. In another large pan, combine tomato sauce, water and bouillon cubes; bring to a boil. Add browned pasta, onion and garlic. Boil until pasta is done.

"Great as a side dish to a Mexican meal or simple meal alone."

Rhonda Prather　　　　　　　　**Joe Walker Middle School, Quartz Hill, CA**

Southwest Citrus Chicken Soup

Serves 8

    4 chicken breast halves, skinless, boneless
    6 cups chicken broth
    1 onion, chopped
    1 (14.5 ounce) can diced tomatoes, undrained
    2 teaspoons lemon peel, grated
    1/2 teaspoon oregano
    1/4 teaspoon pepper
    salt, to taste
    2 red potatoes, scrubbed, diced
    1 cup frozen corn
    1/3 cup cilantro, chopped
    2 fresh mild chiles (Anaheim or New Mexico), seeded, chopped

Rinse chicken and place in soup pot. Add broth, onion, tomatoes, lemon peel, oregano and pepper. Bring to a boil over medium heat. Reduce heat, cover and simmer until chicken is cooked, about 25 minutes. Lift out chicken and set aside. As chicken cools, add potatoes to pan. Cover pan and cook until potatoes are tender, about 25 minutes. Shred cooled chicken into bite-sized pieces. Skim fat from soup. Add chicken, corn, cilantro and chiles. Cook until meat and vegetables are heated through. Salt to taste and adjust seasonings. Note: If a spicier soup is desired, use jalapeño chiles.

"Serve with warm bread or tortillas and a garden salad.
It makes a delicious, healthy dinner."

Wendy Johnson　　　　　　　　**Temecula Valley High School, Temecula, CA**

Southwest Tortellini Chowder

Serves 6

Photo Opposite
Page 128

    3 (10.5 ounce) cans condensed chicken broth
    1 1/2 cups Old El Paso Mild Thick 'n Chunky Salsa or Picante
    1/2 teaspoon orange peel, grated
    2 (9 ounce) packages refrigerated meat-filled or cheese filled tortellini
    1 (1 pound) package Green Giant American Mixtures Frozen Corn,
        Broccoli and Red Peppers
    1 (5 ounce) can evaporated milk
    dash salt
    1/4 cup fresh cilantro, chopped

In Dutch oven or large saucepan, combine broth, salsa and orange peel. Bring to a boil. Reduce heat to low; simmer 3 minutes. Stir in tortellini and vegetables; cook over medium heat for 6 to 8 minutes or until tortellini and vegetables are tender. Stir in milk and salt; cook 1 to 2 minutes or just until thoroughly heated, stirring occasionally. DO NOT BOIL. Top each serving of chowder with cilantro. Note: 1 (16 ounce) package frozen tortellini can be substituted for refrigerated tortellini. Add frozen tortellini to simmered broth mixture; cook 4 minutes. Add vegetables; cook an additional 6 to 8 minutes or until tortellini and vegetables are tender.

Pillsbury Foods   **Minneapolis, MN**

Taco Soup

Serves 6

    1/2 pound hamburger
    1/4 cup onion, chopped
    1 cup water
    1 (16 ounce) can stewed tomatoes
    1 (8 ounce) can tomato sauce
    1 (16 ounce) can kidney beans
    1/2 package taco seasoning
    Garnish: shredded cheddar cheese, corn chips, sour cream

In a large saucepan, cook hamburger and onion until meat is brown; drain off excess fat. Add water, tomatoes, tomato sauce, kidney beans and taco seasoning. Simmer, covered for 30 minutes. Serve with desired garnish.

    "This was shared by Dana Kruse, a member of our faculty, at a soup luncheon
    It's delicious. I usually double the recipe when I make it at home."

Ruth Schletewitz   **Rafer Johnson Junior High School, Kingsburg, CA**

Tex-Mex Chili-Mac Soup

Serves 4

    2 teaspoons vegetable oil
    1 cup bell pepper, chopped
    1 cup onion, chopped
    4 teaspoons jalapeño peppers, chopped
    2 cups tomato puree

2 cups water
2 tablespoons chili powder
1 teaspoon sugar
$1/2$ teaspoon salt
dash pepper
1 pound ground beef, cooked
1 cup elbow macaroni, cooked
4 ounces kidney beans, drained
4 tablespoons sour cream
4 teaspoons parsley, chopped

In a fry pan, cook beef; drain fat and set aside. Prepare macaroni according to package directions; set aside. Heat oil in skillet over medium-high heat, saute pepper, onion and jalapeños for 1 to 2 minutes. Add tomato, water, chili powder, sugar and seasonings, Simmer 2 to 3 minutes. Add remaining ingredients, except sour cream. Simmer for 3 minutes. Garish with sour cream and parsley.

Katrina Brighton　　　　　**Swainston Middle School, North Las Vegas, NV**

Tortilla Soup

Serves 6

1 pound ground sirloin
1 onion, chopped
1 jalapeño pepper, seeded, chopped
3 cloves garlic, minced
2 teaspoons chili powder
2 teaspoons ground cumin
1 (28 ounce) can tomatoes in thick puree
3 cups water
2 (15 ounce) cans pinto beans, drained

Brown ground sirloin with onion and garlic; drain excess fat. Add remaining ingredients except beans and cook 15 minutes. Add beans, cook 10 minutes more.

"This recipe came out of 'Country Living' magazine. It's easy and great tasting. I add cheese and chips when serving."

Donna Swennes　　　　　**El Capitan High School, Lakeside, CA**

Bean Salad With Salsa

Serves 8

    3 (15 to16 ounce) cans beans (red kidney, garbanzo, black or combination),
        rinsed, drained
    1 (8 ounce) can whole kernel corn, drained
    $1/2$ cup jicama, peeled, chopped OR water chestnuts
    $1/3$ cup green onions, sliced
    $3/4$ cup salsa
    $1/3$ cup French or Italian dressing

In a large mixing bowl, combine beans, corn, jicama or water chestnuts and onions.
For the dressing, combine salsa with French or Italian dressing. Pour over
vegetables and toss gently to coat. Cover and refrigerate for 2 to 24 hours. Toss
before serving.

"Great served with barbecued foods! Very easy!"

Judy Hammann　　　　　　　　　　　　　　　**Mesa Junior High School, Mesa, AZ**

Cabo San Lucas Salad

Serves 6

Dressing:
2 jalapeño peppers, chopped
$1/4$ cup mayonnaise
2 tablespoons sour cream
1 tablespoon olive oil
1 tablespoon lime juice
1 clove garlic, minced
$1/4$ teaspoon sugar
$1/4$ teaspoon ground cumin
Salad:
$1/2$ cup jicama, peeled and diced
4 green onions, chopped
mixed salad greens
$1/4$ cup shelled sunflower seeds

Combine dressing ingredients in blender; refrigerate 2 to 3 hours to allow flavors to blend. Combine jicama, onions, and salad greens in large salad bowl. Toss with dressing and sprinkle with sunflower seeds just before serving.

Pam Ford   **Temecula Valley High School, Temecula, CA**

Chicken Fajita Salad

Serves 4 - 6

2 tablespoons cooking oil, divided
$1/4$ cup lime juice
1 clove garlic, minced
$1/2$ teaspoon ground cumin
$1/2$ teaspoon oregano
1 pound boneless skinless chicken breast halves, cut into thin strips
1 onion, cut into thin wedges
1 sweet red pepper, cut into thin strips
1 (7 ounce) can green chiles, diced, drained
1 cup whole almonds, toasted
shredded lettuce
3 tomatoes, cut into wedges
1 avocado, sliced

Combine 1 tablespoon oil, lime juice, garlic, cumin and oregano; toss with chicken; marinate at least 30 minutes. Meanwhile, in a skillet, heat remaining oil over medium-high heat. Saute onion 2 minutes. Drain chicken, reserving marinade. Add chicken to skillet; stir-fry until it begins to brown. Add red pepper, chiles and marinade; cook 2 minutes. Stir in almonds. Serve immediately over shredded lettuce and garnish with tomato wedges and avocado slices.

"This recipe is from Country magazine and we love it!"

Charlotte Heitzmann   **Mariposa County High School, Mariposa, CA**

Christmas Eve Salad

Serves 8

- 2 oranges, peeled and sliced into segments
- 1/2 medium jicama, peeled, cut into 3/4" cubes
- 2 ripe bananas, peeled, sliced
- 1/2 fresh pineapple, cut into 3/4" chunks
- 1 head romaine lettuce, cut into 2" thick slices
- 2 tablespoons lime juice
- 1 teaspoon sugar
- 3 tablespoons orange juice
- 2/3 cup salad oil
- 3/4 cup pine nuts
- 1 (16 ounce) can beets, drained, sliced
- 2 medium red apples, cored, halved , thinly sliced
- 1/2 cup pomegranate seeds (optional)

In a large bowl, gently toss oranges, jicama, bananas and pineapple together making a fruit salad. Arrange romaine on large platter. Gently pile fruit in center of plate. Dressing: Mixing lime juice, sugar and orange juice in food processor or blender. With blender or processor on, slowly add salad oil in a thin stream; mix until creamy. In skillet, sauté pine nuts in 2 tablespoons oil until lightly browned. With remaining dressing, coat beets and drizzle dressing over fruit salad. Arrange apple & beet slices around fruit salad. Sprinkle with pomegranate seeds and pine nuts.

"A beautiful salad for Christmas Eve dinner.
Vary the fruit, but beets, oranges and apples are a traditional part of the salad."
Sharon Turner   **El Dorado High School, Placentia, CA**

Corn Salad

Serves 4

- 1 (12 ounce) can whole kernel corn
- 1/2 medium red onion, chopped
- 1 fresh tomato, chopped
- 1/2 cup green pepper, diced
- 1/2 cup green onion, chopped
- 1/4 cup cilantro leaves, chopped
- 4 tablespoons white vinegar
- 1 tablespoon parsley, chopped
- salt and pepper, to taste
- *Garnish:* avocado slices

In a bowl, combine all ingredients and chill for 30 minutes. Garnish with avocado slices.

"A wonderful zesty salad!"
Sharron Maurice   **Blythe Middle School, Blythe, CA**

Ensenada Shrimp Salad

Serves 4

1 pound medium shrimp, peeled and deveined
2 cloves garlic, minced
2 tablespoons olive oil
$2/3$ cup picante sauce
$1^1/4$ teaspoons ground cumin
$1/2$ teaspoon salt
4 slices bacon, crisply cooked, crumbled
1 tablespoon balsamic vinegar
1 cup celery, sliced
1 cup cherry tomatoes, halved or quartered
$1/2$ cup green onions, with tops, sliced
lettuce leaves
1 ripe avocado, peeled, sliced

In 10" skillet, cook shrimp and garlic in oil 2 minutes. Add picante saute and simmer, uncovered until shrimp are cooked through, about 4 minutes. Remove shrimp to large bowl with slotted spoon. Add cumin and salt to skillet, continue to simmer until mixture is slightly thickened, about 2 minutes. Remove from heat, stir in bacon and vinegar. Pour over shrimp; toss. Cover and chill. Add celery, tomatoes and green onions, cover and chill. To serve, arrange lettuce on serving platter or individual plates, top with shrimp mixture. Arrange slices of avocado over shrimp mixture and serve with additional picante sauce.

Peggy Herndon　　　　　**Central Valley High School, Shasta Lake City, CA**

Guacamole Tomato Salad

Serves 2

2 cups Bibb or Boston lettuce
1 medium tomato, cut into wedges or sliced
$1/2$ medium cucumber, sliced
1 tablespoon lime juice
1 tablespoon olive oil
1 tablespoon honey
$1/4$ teaspoon salt
2 tablespoons guacamole, prepared
few sprigs cilantro, for garnish

In medium bowl, combine lettuce, tomato and cucumber slices, toss. In small bowl, combine remaining ingredients; blend well. Spoon salad onto individual salad plates; drizzle with dressing. Garnish with cilantro.

"This recipe is great for 'empty nesters' that really enjoy cooking but hate to make large portions."

Dotti Jones　　　　　**Etiwanda High School, Etiwanda, CA**

Jicama Salad

Serves 4

> 1 1/2 cups jicama, peeled and cubed
> 1 large cucumber, sliced
> 1 orange, peeled, diced
> 2 tablespoons lemon juice
> 3/4 teaspoon chili powder

In serving dish, combine jicama, cucumber and oranges, Sprinkle with lemon juice and chili powder; toss. Cover and chill at least 2 hours. Just before serving, sprinkle lightly with salt (and additional chili powder if desired) and toss.

"Refreshing and light!"

April Rosendahl   **Chino High School, Chino, CA**

Mexican Cole Slaw

Serves 12 - 14

> 2 (15 ounce) cans kidney beans, rinsed, drained
> 1 cup oil
> 1 cup garlic flavored wine vinegar
> 1 teaspoon salt
> 1/8 teaspoon black pepper
> 1/8 teaspoon garlic salt
> 1 tablespoon sugar
> dash red pepper
> 1 head cabbage, shredded
> 6 stalks celery, sliced
> 1 green bell pepper, minced
> 1 bunch green onions, minced

Combine kidney beans with oil, vinegar, salt, pepper, garlic salt, sugar and red pepper; set aside. In large bowl, toss cabbage, celery, green pepper and green onions. Stir in kidney bean mixture with cabbage and chill; stirring once or twice.

"Great flavor."

Ginny Clark   **Sonora High School, La Habra, CA**

Mexican Crab Tostadas

Serves 4

> 1 large avocado, peeled, pitted
> 2 tablespoons lime juice
> 1/4 teaspoon garlic salt
> 1 large head iceberg lettuce
> 2 1/2 cups refried beans
> 4 corn tortillas, fried crisp
> 1 cup mild cheddar cheese, shredded
> 3/4 to 1 pound crab, cooked
> 2 (medium-sized) tomatoes, sliced

1/2 cup ripe olives, pitted
taco sauce or salsa

Mash avocados and blend with lime juice and garlic salt. Line four dinner plates with outer leaves of lettuce; then finely shred remaining lettuce and mound on plates. Heat beans until they start to bubble. Arrange a crisp tortilla atop greens and spoon over hot beans. Sprinkle with cheese and cover with a layer of crab, reserving some crab for garnish. Spoon on avocado mixture; garnish with reserved crab, tomato slices and olives. Pass taco sauce or salsa to spoon over all.

"This is delicious with our local Dungeness crab at Christmas time."

Pam Cahill   **Eureka High School, Eureka, CA**

Nopalitos Salad

Serves 6

2 cups tender cactus (Embasa Nopalitos)
3 green onions, chopped
5 large radishes, chopped
2 Serrano chiles, diced
1 tomato, diced
3/4 cup fresh cilantro, chopped
juice from 1 lemon
1/2 teaspoon salt

In large bowl, combine cactus, green onions, radishes, chiles, tomato and cilantro. Squeeze lemon over and sprinkle with salt. Serve.

"This is an original creation of a very special friend, Eduwiges Perez."

Mary M. Rector   **Valley High School, Las Vegas, NV**

Orange Onion Pine Nut Salad (OOPS)

Serves 4

1 head romaine lettuce
1 can Mandarin oranges, drained
1 red onion, sliced, separated into rings
1/2 cup pint nuts, toasted
Dressing:
1/4 cup sugar
1/4 cup vinegar, or juice from Mandarin oranges
1/2 cup salad oil

In large salad bowl, mix together lettuce, oranges, onion and pine nuts. Mix dressing ingredients together and pour over salad. Toss gently and serve.

Sue Walters   **Morse High School, San Diego, CA**

Ranch Taco Chicken Salad

Serves 6

    1 tablespoon cooking oil
    1 pound chicken breast, boneless, skinless, cut into strips
    1 tablespoon chili powder
    salad greens
    1 cup cheddar cheese, shredded
    8 ounces salsa
    1 (8 ounce) bottle Ranch dressing
    1/2 cup tortilla chips, crushed

Heat oil in large skillet on medium-high heat. Cook chicken, sprinkled with chili powder for 8 minutes or until cooked through. Remove from pan. Toss chicken with salad greens and cheese in large bowl. Top with salsa, salad dressing and crushed chips just before serving.

Olga Sarouhan   **Edison High School, Huntington Beach, CA**

Rice Taco Salad

Serves 6

    1 pound ground beef
    1/2 onion, finely chopped
    1 clove garlic, minced
    1/2 teaspoon salt
    1/2 teaspoon ground cumin
    1/4 teaspoon ground black pepper
    3 cups rice, cooked
    1/2 head lettuce, shredded
    2 tomatoes, coarsely chopped
    1/2 cup cheddar cheese, shredded
    1 large avocado, peeled, seeded, diced
    1/4 cup sour cream

Photo Opposite
Page 65

Cook meat over medium-high heat until browned in large skillet; stirring to crumble. Add onion and garlic; cook until soft but not brown. Drain fat. Add salt, cumin, pepper and rice. Remove from heat; cool. Combine lettuce, tomatoes, cheese, avocado and rice mixture in large bowl. Add sour cream and toss lightly. Serve immediately with picante sauce and corn chips, if desired.

USA Rice Council   **Houston, TX**

Sombrero Salad

Serves 8

    Fluffy Dressing:
    1/3 cup sugar
    1 tablespoon flour
    1 teaspoon lemon peel, grated
    1/4 cup lemon juice
    1 egg, beaten

1 cup marshmallows, halved
1/2 pint sour cream
Coconut Bananas:
4 bananas, peeled
4 tablespoons lemon juice
1 pint sour cream
1 1/2 cups coconut, shredded
Salad:
1 sombrero (Mexican hat)
1 medium pineapple, cut in wedges, reserve top
1/2 small watermelon
1 cantaloupe
1/2 honeydew melon
1 to 2 pints strawberries, washed
2 bunches green grapes
2 bunches purple grapes
mint sprigs, for garnish

Prepare dressing: In large saucepan combine sugar and flour; stir in lemon peel, lemon juice and egg, mixing until smooth. Add marshmallows. Stir over low heat until thickened slightly, 10 to 15 minutes. Cool. Stir in sour cream. Refrigerate (can be refrigerated several days). Prepare coconut bananas: Cut bananas into 1" pieces. Place lemon juice, sour cream and coconut in separate bowls. Dip banana pieces in lemon juice. Roll in sour cream, then in coconut, making sure all sides are coated. Cover with plastic wrap and refrigerate several hours or overnight.

To arrange salad: Place sombrero on platter. Secure top of pineapple in the peak of sombrero with skewers or turkey lacers. Line the base of a sombrero with plastic wrap. Cut watermelon, cantaloupe and honeydew melons into serving size pieces. (A fluted French fry cutter works exceptionally well.) Place coconut bananas and other fruit attractively around sombrero's base. Garnish with sprigs of mint. Using straight pins, hang small clusters of grapes at random from top of sombrero. Serve with Fluffy Dressing. Note: if your refrigerator can accommodate it, assemble the salad a day ahead. Cover with damp paper towels and plastic wrap.

"From Cookery for Entertaining, *by Marlene Sorosky. A great edible centerpiece!"*
Pat Dallas   **Westminster High School, Westminster, CA**

Southwestern Shrimp Salad

Serves 8

4 cups pasta, cooked
1/2 red bell pepper, diced
1 avocado, peeled, diced
1/2 pound shrimp, cooked
Dressing:
2/3 cup mayonnaise
1/2 cup cilantro, chopped
2 tablespoons lime juice
1/2 teaspoon salt
dash pepper
5 drops Tabasco
Garnish: cherry tomatoes

Prepare pasta according to package directions. In large bowl, combine pasta with bell pepper, avocado and shrimp; set aside. Blend together dressing ingredients and toss with pasta. Garnish with tomatoes.

"This is a delightful salad for cilantro and shrimp lovers."

Connie Halloway   **Rubidoux High School, Rubidoux, CA**

Taco Salad

Serves 6 - 8

> 1 pound ground beef
> 1 (16 ounce) can tomato sauce
> salt and pepper, to taste
> 1 tablespoon minced onion
> 1 teaspoon garlic powder
> 1 tablespoon chili powder
> 1 head lettuce, shredded
> 1 (2.2 ounce) can olives, chopped, drained
> 1 pound cheddar cheese, shredded
> 3 tomatoes, chopped
> 1 (10 ounce) bag corn chips

Brown ground beef with tomato sauce and seasonings; drain excess fat and discard; cool. Toss together lettuce, olives, cheese and tomatoes. Add cooled meat. Just before serving, toss with corn chips.

"Always popular at any gathering!"

Gaylen Roe   **Magnolia Junior High School, Chino, CA**

Tex-Mex Turkey & Rice Salad

Serves 4

> 1 1/2 cups turkey or chicken, cooked, shredded
> 2 cups rice, cooked
> 1/2 cup frozen corn kernels, thawed
> 1/2 cup celery, diced
> 1/2 cup red bell pepper, diced
> 1 teaspoon ground cumin
> 1 teaspoon chili powder
> 1 teaspoon dried oregano
> 1 tablespoon oil
> 1 tablespoon water
> 1/2 teaspoon hot pepper sauce
> 2 tablespoons cilantro, chopped
> 12 to 16 Boston lettuce leaves
> *Garnish:* cilantro leaves

Mix turkey or chicken, rice, corn, celery and red pepper in a 2 quart bowl. In a small bowl, combine cumin, chili powder, oregano, oil, water, hot pepper sauce and chopped cilantro. Pour over turkey mixture and toss until well combined. Chill at least 4 hours or overnight. Stir well before serving; adjust seasonings and hot sauce. To serve, arrange lettuce leaves on serving platter. (If desired, warm salad in microwave oven on medium-power for 2 minutes.) Spoon salad into center of platter. Garnish with cilantro leaves.

Clyle Alt   **Bell Gardens High School, Bell Gardens, CA**

Tortilla Cup Meat Salad

Serves 4

    4 (8") flour tortillas
    1 pound boneless beef sirloin or chicken, thinly sliced
    $1/4$ teaspoon garlic powder
    $1/4$ teaspoon salt
    1 tablespoon vegetable oil
    $1/2$ cup picante sauce
    $1/3$ cup prepared Italian salad dressing
    2 green onions, chopped
    1 to 2 tomatoes, sliced or 1 $1/2$ cups cherry tomatoes
    $1/2$ cup mushrooms, thinly sliced (optional)
    $1/2$ cup baby carrots, thinly sliced (optional)
    5 cups salad greens, torn into bite-sized pieces
    Garnish: sliced olives, avocado slices

Preheat oven to 400 degrees. In shallow-sided baking dish, place 4 (4 ounce) custard cups upside down. Soften tortillas in microwave 2 at a time for 20 seconds. Drape a tortilla over each cup, scalloping the edges. Bake 10 minutes or until edges are golden. Remove from oven and cool. Toss beef or chicken with garlic powder and salt. In medium skillet over medium-high heat, heat oil. Stir fry meat until browned; remove to a bowl. To skillet, add picante sauce, dressing, onions, tomatoes, mushrooms and baby carrots; heat to a boil. Return meat to pan and heat through. Arrange 1 $1/4$ cups greens in each tortilla cup with meat mixture. Garnish.

Betty Byrne   **Vaca Peña Middle School, Vacaville, CA**

Walking Taco Salad

Serves 12

    1 large can "Spicy" refried beans
    1 (16 ounce) carton sour cream
    1 frozen carton avocado dip, thawed
    3 green onions, finely chopped
    3 tomatoes, chopped
    1 (8.5 ounce) can olives, chopped
    1 (7 ounce) can green chiles, diced
    1 (15 ounce) jar salsa
    1 $1/2$ pounds mild cheddar and jack cheese (combined) , shredded
    1 large bag tortilla chips

Spread beans over bottom of a large platter, top with sour cream, then avocado dip. Garnish liberally with remaining ingredients (except tortilla chips) and refrigerate until ready to serve. Serve with tortilla chips.

"Recipe is best with Rosarita spicy refried beans."

Mary Tatro-Davis   **Lakeview Junior High School, Orcutt, CA**

Wild Spinach Salad

Serves 1

- 1 handful spinach
- 1 handful dandelion greens
- 1 small red onion, sliced
- 4 mushrooms, sliced
- 1 hard boiled egg, peeled, sliced

Dressing:
- 2 tablespoons red wine vinegar
- 2 tablespoons bacon drippings
- 2 tablespoons vegetable oil
- 1 clove garlic, pressed

Combine salad ingredients in a large bowl. Stir together dressing ingredients and pour over salad. Toss gently and serve.

Pat Sellers   **Morse High School, San Diego, CA**

Tostada Salad

Serves 8 - 10

- 1 large package Doritos chips
- 1 pound ground beef, browned and drained
- 3/4 teaspoon Lawry's Seasoned Salt
- 1 cup chopped onion
- 1 (8 - 12 oz.) can refried beans, heated
- 4 ounces cheddar cheese, grated
- 1 head of lettuce, torn into small pieces
- 4 tomatoes, diced
- 1 (6 - 8 oz.) container frozen avocado dip, thawed
- 1 pint sour cream
- salsa

Heat Doritos chips in the oven at 350 degrees for 15 minutes. Assemble each plate by placing a serving of Doritos on the plate. Top with ground beef, then onion, refried beans, cheese, lettuce, and tomatoes. Top with avocado and sour cream. Add salsa, if desired.

"This is a great meal to serve in the summer... easy to make.
Everyone likes it, young and old... light eaters and heavy eaters.
Let everyone assemble their own plate."

Gage Hewes   **South Pasadena High School, South Pasadena, CA**

Braided Bread

Makes 1 loaf

> 2 packages dry active yeast
> 1/4 cup lukewarm water
> 2 eggs
> 1 1/2 teaspoons salt
> 2 tablespoons sugar
> 1 cup water
> 1/4 teaspoon yellow food coloring
> 4 cups flour
> 1 egg yolk, mixed with 1 teaspoon water
> poppy seeds

Dissolve yeast in lukewarm water in a large bowl. Add eggs, salt, sugar, water, food coloring, and 2 cups of the flour; mix well. Add remaining flour and knead until elastic. Cover and set in a warm place to rise until doubled in size. Divide dough into 3 parts. Roll each part into a long rope; braid the 3 ropes together and place on a well-greased cookie sheet. Let rise until doubled in size, (about 1 to 1 1/4 hours). Brush top lightly with egg yolk and water. Sprinkle with poppy seeds. Bake in preheated 375 degree oven for 30 minutes.

"This recipe is great eaten by itself or with a meal!"

Nancy Patten   **Placerita Junior High School, Santa Clarita, CA**

Buñuelos or Sopaipillas

Serves 8

3/4 teaspoon salt
1 teaspoon baking powder
4 cups flour
2 eggs
1 cup milk
oil, for deep frying

Sift dry ingredients together. Beat eggs well; add milk. Stir in dry ingredients, adding more flour if needed until soft dough forms. Roll as thin as possible. Cut in small squares to make sopaipillas. Cut large and round with a hole pinched in the middle to make bunuelos. Fry in deep fryer until they turn a delicate brown.

"Traditionally these are served with honey and Mexican chocolate at 4 in the afternoon."

Karen McCord   **Lindsay High School, Lindsay, CA**

Churros Muffins

Makes 12

Muffins:
1/3 cup shortening
1/2 cup sugar
1 egg
1 1/2 cups flour
1 1/2 teaspoons baking powder
1/2 teaspoon salt
1/4 teaspoon nutmeg
1/2 cup milk
Topping:
1/3 cup butter
1 teaspoon cinnamon
1/2 cup sugar

Preheat oven to 350 degrees. Line muffin pan with paper liners. Cream together shortening, sugar and egg. In another bowl, sift together flour, baking powder, salt and nutmeg. Add 1/2 of the sifted ingredients to the creamed mixture; stir. Add milk; stir. Add remaining dry ingredients and stir until batter is formed. Fill muffin cups 2/3 full and bake 15 to 20 minutes. Remove from oven to cool. In small, flat bowl or pie plate, melt butter in microwave. Mix cinnamon and sugar together in another small, flat bowl or pie plate. Remove paper from muffins and roll in melted butter, then in cinnamon-sugar.

"These are a classroom favorite! They are wonderful served warm from the oven!"

Sue Campbell   **Chico Junior High School, Chico, CA**

Fiesta Bread

Serves 8

> 2/3 cup milk
> 2 cup Bisquick mix
> 2 tablespoons butter or margarine, melted
> 3 to 4 tomatoes, sliced
> salt and pepper, to taste
> 1 cup sour cream
> 2/3 cup mayonnaise
> 1 cup cheddar cheese, shredded
> 1 medium onion, finely chopped
> paprika

Preheat oven to 325 degrees. Combine milk with Bisquick mix, stirring to form a soft dough. Knead a few times on floured bread board. Roll into rectangle and fit into a greased 9" x 12" x 2" pan. Push dough up sides to form a slight crust and brush with melted butter or margarine. Arrange sliced tomatoes in rows over dough, salt and pepper, to taste. Combine sour cream, mayonnaise, cheddar cheese and onion. Spoon evenly over tomatoes. Sprinkle with paprika. Bake 20 to 25 minutes.

"Quick, simple and delicious."

Vernae Kajiya   **Schurr High School, Montebello, CA**

Flour Tortillas

Makes 12

> 3 cups flour
> 1/2 teaspoon baking powder
> 1/2 teaspoon salt
> 2 tablespoons oil
> hot water (to make dough smooth)

Combine dry ingredients; add oil. Begin adding enough hot water to make a smooth dough. Knead dough about 1 minute; let rest. Divide dough into small balls. Roll each ball into thin circle. Cook on a hot, dry griddle, each side about 30 seconds, until bubbly. Turn and cook until done, about 1 minute.

"This recipe is also authentic and from the students.
Very light and delicious. Often the students don't measure."

Joan Wayland   **O.W. Holmes Junior High School, Davis, CA**

Kid's Tortillas

Serves 4

> 1 1/4 cups whole grain flour
> 1/4 cup butter
> 5/8 cup warm water
> olive oil

Sift flour into a bowl. Add butter, cutting into pea-sized pieces. Stir in water. Mix into a dough. Divide dough into 12 balls. Brush each ball with oil, cover and let set

20 minutes. Roll each ball into a 5 1/2" circle. Brush a heavy pan with oil. Cook tortillas gently on medium-high heat for 2 minutes on each side. Add your favorite toppings and enjoy!

"My son, Carl, can't make enough of these tortillas!
He'll ask me every day if he can make "circles"!"

Kathleen Yonter   **Burkholder Middle School, Henderson, NV**

Mexican Spoon Bread

Serves 4

        1 cup flour
        1 cup cornmeal
        1/2 teaspoon baking soda
        1 teaspoon salt
        1/3 cup shortening
        1 can creamed corn
        3/4 cup milk
        2 eggs, beaten
        1 (4 ounce) can green chiles, diced
        1 1/2 pound cheddar or jack cheese, shredded

Mix together flour, cornmeal, baking soda and salt in a bowl; cut in shortening. Add remaining ingredients. Mix just until moistened, being careful not to overmix. Bake at 300 degrees for 35 to 45 minutes. Just before serving, top with more shredded cheese, if desired.

Becky Pfeiffer   **McLane High School, Fresno, CA**

Smokey Cheese Chile Muffins

Makes 10

        1 cup all-purpose flour
        1 cup cornmeal
        1 tablespoon baking powder
        1/2 teaspoon salt
        1 (8 ounce) can Dole Crushed Pineapple, drained
        1 whole egg, beaten
        1 egg white, beaten
        1/2 cup lowfat at milk
        1/4 cup vegetable oil
        1/4 cup green chiles, diced
        1 1/4 cups smoked Cheddar cheese, finely chopped
        nonstick cooking spray

Photo Opposite
Page 128

Combine flour, cornmeal, baking powder and salt in large bowl. In a medium bowl, combine pineapple, egg, egg white, milk, oil and chiles. Stir into dry mixture just until moistened. Stir in cheese. Spoon batter into paper lined muffin cups coated with nonstick cooking spray. Bake at 400 degrees for 18 to 20 minutes, until toothpick inserted comes out clean.

Dole Foods   **San Francisco, CA**

Sopaipillas (with yeast)

Serves 12

2 cups flour, sifted
3/4 teaspoon salt
1/2 teaspoon baking powder
1 1/2 teaspoons shortening
1 1/2 teaspoons active dry yeast (1/2 package)
2 tablespoons warm water
1/2 cup + 2 tablespoons scalded milk
oil, for frying
powdered sugar, for topping

Combine dry ingredients and cut in shortening. Dissolve yeast in lukewarm water. Scald milk by bringing milk to a point where it just begins to steam; cool to room temperature. Add cooled, scalded milk to yeast and water. Make a well in center of dry ingredients. Add liquid ingredients and work into a soft dough. Knead dough 15 to 20 times and set aside for 10 minutes (or refrigerate overnight at this point). Roll dough to 1/4" thickness and cut into 1" squares. Fry in hot oil; drain and dust with powdered sugar. Serve. Note: If oil is not hot enough, sopaipillas; will puff up and become hollow.

"Wonderful, because of the yeast. From a little cookbook called Cocinas de New Mexico, *by the Public Service Co. of New Mexico."*

Sue Overmire   **Prospect High School, Saratoga, CA**

Spanish Cornbread

Serves 6

1 1/2 cups corn bread mix
2 eggs
1/2 cup oil
1 cup sour cream
2 tablespoons minced onion
1 cup cream-style corn
1 (4 ounce) green chiles, diced

Preheat oven to 350 degrees. In a mixing bowl, combine all ingredients, stirring to mix well. Pour into a greased 9" x 13" pan. Bake 30 to 35 minutes.

"Not hot, just a bit of zing! Great for a chef's salad dinner."

Jean Hanson   **Red Bluff High School, Red Bluff, CA**

VEGETABLES & SIDE DISHES

Arroz Con Jocoque

Serves 6

- 3/4 pound jack cheese
- 3 cups sour cream
- 2 cups green chiles, diced
- 3 cups cooked rice
- 1/2 cup cheddar cheese, shredded

Cut jack cheese into strips. Mix together sour cream and chiles. Butter a 1 1/2 quart casserole. Layer rice, sour cream mixture and cheese strips; repeat, finishing with rice on top. Bake, covered at 350 degrees for 1 1/2 hours. During last few minutes of baking, sprinkle with cheddar cheese.

"A delicious and easy rice recipe—my family loves it!"

Priscilla M. Rogers   **Wilson High School, Long Beach, CA**

Aunt Dixie's Creamy Chile Rice

Serves 4

  1/4 cup green chiles, diced
  1/2 cup sour cream
  1 tablespoon green onion, chopped
  1/2 teaspoon salt
  1 cup cooked rice
  1/2 cup jack cheese, shredded
  1 tomato, sliced
  1/4 cup Parmesan cheese, grated

In a small bowl, mix together chiles, sour cream, green onion and salt. Place 1/2 cup rice in a lightly buttered 8" or 9" pie pan. Spoon 1/2 of the sour cream mixture over rice. Sprinkle with 1/2 cup jack cheese. Repeat layers and top with sliced tomato and Parmesan cheese. Bake 12 minutes, or until cheese melts and begins to bubble.

"Pour this in a baked pie crust for a Mexican Quiche or skip the crust and use nonfat sour cream and nonfat cheese for a lower calorie version."

Larkin Evans   **Half Moon Bay High School, Half Moon Bay, CA**

Authentic Spanish Rice

Serves 6

  2 tablespoon oil
  1 cup rice
  1 clove garlic, minced
  2 tablespoons onion
  4 ounces tomato sauce
  2 cups cold water
  1/2 teaspoon salt
  1 cube chicken bouillon

Coat bottom of saucepan with oil and saute rice until golden brown; drain excess oil. Add garlic to rice and saute for 1 minute. Add tomato sauce, water, salt and chicken bouillon and stir well to mix ingredients. Bring to a boil, stirring occasionally. Lower heat to simmer. Cover and simmer for 25 minutes.

"Been making this for generations...delicious!"

Adriana Molinaro   **Granite Hills High School, El Cajon, CA**

Bacon-Refried Beans

Serves 6 - 8

  1 pound bacon, chopped into small pieces
  1 medium onion, chopped
  2 (20 ounce) cans pinto beans
  salsa
  salt and pepper

In large frying pan, fry bacon until done but not crisp. To bacon and grease, add onions and saute until translucent. Add beans with liquid to pot and mash with wooden spoon. Season with salsa, salt and pepper.

"These beans are quick and easy and people rave about them! You can lighten up this recipe by taking out some of the grease–but leave some for the taste!"

Michelle Garewal   **Los Banos High School, Los Banos, CA**

Cheesy Bacon Spanish Rice

Serves 8 - 10

    4 slices bacon
    1 cup onion, chopped
    1/2 cup green pepper, diced
    1 (16 ounce) can tomatoes, chopped
    water
    1 (8 ounce) can tomato sauce
    1 teaspoon salt
    1 1/2 cups long grain rice, uncooked
    1/2 cup cheddar cheese, shredded

Fry bacon until crispy. Remove from pan, drain and crumble into pieces. Preheat oven to 350 degrees. In bacon drippings, cook onion and green pepper until tender. Drain tomatoes, reserving liquid. Add enough water to the liquid to make 1 3/4 cups. Add liquid, tomatoes, tomato sauce and salt to onion mixture. Heat to boiling. Stir in rice. Remove from heat and pour into greased 1-1/2 quart casserole. Cover and bake at 350 degrees for 35 minutes or until rice is tender and liquid is absorbed. Fluff rice with fork; sprinkle with cheese and bake 5 minutes more. Garnish with bacon.

"One of my favorite rice dishes because the rice cooks itself while in the oven."

Jeanette Atkinson   **Cheyenne High School, Las Vegas, NV**

Chili Corn Pudding

Serves 8

    1/2 cup margarine
    1 1/2 cups Bisquick
    2 eggs
    1 (15.5 ounce) can creamed corn
    1/2 cup milk
    1 (4 ounce) can green chiles, whole, sliced open, seeded
    3/4 cup Monterey Jack cheese, shredded

In a large bowl, cut margarine into Bisquick. Add eggs, corn and milk; mix together until moist. Pour 1/2 of batter into a greased 8" x 8" x 2" pan, preferably glass. Cover with a layer of chiles and cheese. Pour remaining batter over top. Bake at 400 degrees for 45 minutes to 1 hour, until set.

"Some people say this tastes similar to chile rellenos."

Monica Carlson   **La Contenta Junior High School, Yucca Valley, CA**

Arroz Con Pollo Burritos
Rice and chicken, a great filling!
Page 103

Rice Taco Salad
Low-fat version of a
traditional favorite!
Page 52

Chorizo Patties

Makes 10 patties

    1 pound lean ground pork
    1 teaspoon salt
    1 to 2 tablespoons chili powder
    $1/4$ teaspoon cloves, ground
    $1/2$ teaspoon cinnamon
    $1/2$ to 1 tablespoon paprika
    1 clove garlic, minced
    1 teaspoon oregano
    $1/4$ teaspoon water

Combine all ingredients and mix well. Refrigerate for several hours. Mix again and shape into small patties. Pan fry at medium-high for 20-30 minutes or until pork is thoroughly cooked.

"Nice alternative to sausage for breakfast. A real treat when Mom made it!"

Maria Montemagni   **Strathmore High School, Strathmore, CA**

Colache

Serves 6

    2 tablespoons margarine
    4 small zucchini, sliced
    1 small onion, chopped
    1 green bell pepper, chopped
    1 $1/2$ cups corn, frozen
    $1/2$ cup water
    1 large tomato, diced
    salt and pepper, to taste

Heat margarine in skillet; stir in zucchini, onion, bell pepper, corn and water. Cover and cook, stirring frequently, about 6 minutes. Mix in tomato and cook, covered, about 3 to 4 minutes more or until vegetables are tender; stir occasionally. Season with salt and pepper.

"Nice vegetable dish to serve with barbecued meats and Mexican food.
Leftovers make great omelet filling sprinkled with a little cheddar cheese!"

Penny Niadna   **Golden West High School, Visalia, CA**

Corn and Zucchini Mexicana

Serves 6 - 8

    2 pounds zucchini, sliced
    1 large onion, chopped
    2 tablespoons butter
    2 (10 ounce) packages frozen corn
    $1/2$ pound Olde English processed cheese, cubed or grated
    1 (4 ounce) can green chiles, diced, seeded
    salt and pepper, to taste

Saute squash and onion in butter until just tender. In another saucepan, cook corn until tender. Add corn, cheese and green chiles to squash and onions. Cook over low heat until cheese is melted, stirring occasionally. Season with salt and pepper. Pour into a 2 quart casserole and bake, uncovered, at 350 degrees for 30 minutes.

"A simple and easy way to use all the summer garden squash."

Nina Hanna   **Roosevelt Junior High School, Modesto, CA**

Frijoles de la Olla

Serves 8

> 2 cups dried pink (pinto) beans
> 1 medium onion, chopped
> 3 cloves garlic, minced
> 1/3 cup bacon drippings
> 1 1/2 teaspoon salt
> 1 (8 ounce) can tomato sauce
> 1 1/2 teaspoon chili powder
> 1/4 teaspoon ground cumin

Cover beans generously with hot tap water and soak overnight. Next morning, drain beans and place them in a large pot; cover with hot water. Add remaining ingredients and bring to a boil. Lower heat and cook slowly, loosely covered, about 3 hours or until beans are tender and a rich sauce is formed. Add more hot water if needed. Beans should be neither too dry or too soupy.

Carol O'Keefe   **Canyon High School, Anaheim Hills, CA**

Green Chile Hash Browns

Serves 8

> 1 (32 ounce) bag frozen hash browns
> 3 (4 ounce) cans green chiles, diced, drained
> 1 (10.75 ounce) can cream of chicken soup
> 2 cups sharp cheddar cheese, shredded
> 1 cup sour cream

Preheat oven to 400 degrees. Stir together all ingredients in large bowl and blend . Transfer mixture to a 13" x 9" x 2" glass baking dish. Cover with foil and bake 30 minutes. Uncover and bake 30 minutes more or until top is golden brown. Serve hot.

"This is a delicious accompaniment dish, especially for breakfast or brunch. I use reduced fat soup and sour cream to lower calorie count."

Doris L. Oitzman   **Victor Valley High School, Victorville, CA**

Grilled Corn with Cotija Cheese

Serves 6

> 6 ears fresh sweet corn, unhusked
> 2 quarts salted water
> 6 teaspoons unrefined corn oil or extra virgin olive oil

2 to 3 tablespoons pickling liquid from jar of pickled jalapeños
1/2 teaspoon cumin seeds, toasted, ground
1/4 teaspoon salt
3 to 4 tablespoons mayonnaise
1/4 pound cotija cheese, crumbled
chili powder, to taste

Remove any loose husks from corn. Pull husks back carefully almost to their base and remove the silk. Slice off tip of corn if is unattractive or undeveloped. Pull husks back up and soak corn in water for 10 to 20 minutes. In a jar with tight fitting lid, combine oil, pickling liquid, cumin and salt. (Mixture should taste hot and sharp but will mellow when slathered over corn.) Pour into serving dish and set aside. On outdoor grill, fire up enough charcoal to make a single layer under the ears. When coals are covered in gray ash, place the corn, fully encased in husks, directly on coals. Grill corn, turning once or twice, until husks are somewhat browned and corn is soft, about 20 minutes. Remove from coals and pull husks back down to expose kernels. Don't remove husks; they provide a handle at one end and add a rustic look. Serve hot with pickling juice or slather with mayonnaise, then sprinkle with cotija cheese crumbles and chili powder to taste.

"At one time, my student's grandmother compared the taste of grilled corn to that of chestnuts. Try it and see what you think."
Stephanie San Sebastian   **Central High School, Fresno, CA**

Jalapeño Corn
Serves 8

1 can whole kernel corn, drained
1 can creamed corn
1 (8 ounce) carton sour cream
1 package jalapeño cornbread mix

Blend all ingredients together in mixing bowl. Lightly grease a baking dish. Pour mixture into baking dish and bake at 350 degrees 45 to 50 minutes.

"My husband's mother, Esther Bundy, shared this recipe with me about twenty years ago and it has been a surprise success with a variety of main dishes."
Betty Bundy   **Hidden Valley Middle School, Escondido, CA**

Jalapeño Jelly
Makes 5 (1/2) pints

6 jalapeño peppers
1 cup white vinegar
4 green bell peppers, finely chopped
4 1/2 cups sugar
1 bottle liquid pectin

Remove seeds and veins from jalapeños. (Use rubber gloves to avoid skin irritation.) In saucepan, combine vinegar, jalapeños, bell peppers and sugar and slowly bring to a boil over medium heat; boil gently 10 minutes. Remove from heat; add liquid pectin and return to heat. Boil on high for 1 minute. Pour into sterilized 1/2 pint jars to within 1/2" of top. Put cap on firmly. Process 5 minutes in a boiling water bath.

"This is excellent served with any meat, or poured on an 8" block of cream cheese and served with crackers as an appetizer."

Rose Varney **Mariposa County High School, Mariposa, CA**

Jalapeño Mashed Potatoes

Serves 4

    1 pound Yukon Gold potatoes
    1 teaspoon olive oil
    1 cup red onion, sliced
    2 cloves garlic crushed
    1 medium jalapeño pepper, seeded, diced
    2 tablespoons lowfat sour cream
    1/4 cup fresh cilantro, chopped
    salt and pepper, to taste

Wash and cut potatoes into 2" pieces. Place in saucepan and cover with cold water. Bring to a boil and boil 15 to 20 minutes, until tender. While potatoes are cooking, heat olive oil over medium heat in nonstick skillet, Saute onion, garlic and jalapeño pepper 5 to 10 minutes. Drain potatoes and mash (using a ricer or food processor, etc.). With a fork, combine potatoes and onion mixture. Stir in sour cream and cilantro; mix well. Salt and pepper, to taste.

"I like the extra zest in this dish!"

Darlene Lupul **Tokay High School, Lodi, CA**

Lowfat Mexican Rice

Serves 8

    2 tablespoons vegetable oil
    2 cups uncooked rice
    3 cups chicken broth
    1 1/2 cups onion, finely chopped
    2 teaspoons garlic, minced
    1 (14.5 ounce) can Mexican style tomatoes
    1/2 teaspoon salt
    1 green pepper, seeded, chopped

Heat oil over medium-high heat and saute rice until golden, about 5 minutes. Add 1/2 cup broth, onion and garlic and saute for 2 minutes. Stir in tomatoes and their liquid, remaining broth, salt and green pepper. Bring to a boil; reduce heat to low. Simmer, covered 20 to 25 minutes or until broth is absorbed.

"This is a lowfat version. It was a big winner with students."

Rita Blohm **Nogales High School, La Puente, CA**
Jan Neufeld **Fullerton High School, Fullerton, CA**
Libby Newman **West Valley High School, Hemet, CA**
Janet Riegel **Charter Oak High School, Covina, CA**

Macarena Macaroni

Serves 4

>   2 cups elbow macaroni
>   1 block Velveeta cheese, cubed
>   1 1/2 to 2 cups milk
>   1 tablespoon margarine
>   *Garnish:* 1 cup sour cream mixed with 2 tablespoons taco seasoning, salsa,
>   chopped cilantro

Cook macaroni until tender. Meanwhile, melt cheese in microwave safe dish in microwave. Stir in milk and margarine and heat 1 to 1 1/2 minutes more. Drain macaroni, stir in cheese sauce. At this point, it may be put into oven at low temperature until ready to serve or serve immediately. Before serving, mix together sour cream and taco seasoning; use as garnish.

>   *"This is a great alternative to Spanish rice as a side dish to*
>   *just about anything like enchiladas, tacos or chimichangas."*

Linda Heinbach   **Yosemite High School, Oakhurst, CA**

Mexican Potatoes au Gratin

Serves 8

>   2 pounds Ore-Ida hash browns
>   2 pounds Mexican Velveeta cheese, hot, cut into 1/2" cubes
>   1 (16 ounce) carton sour cream
>   1 can cream of chicken soup
>   chili powder

Mix all ingredients together in a 9" x 13" pan. Sprinkle with chili powder. Bake at 325 degrees for 45 to 55 minutes.

>   *"Really really really good!"*

Elizabeth DeMars   **West Hills High School, Santee, CA**

Rice Ortega

Serves 8

>   1/2 cup onion, chopped
>   1 bay leaf
>   2 tablespoons butter or margarine
>   4 cups rice, cooked
>   1 cup cottage cheese
>   2 cups sour cream
>   1 (4 ounce) can green chiles, diced
>   2 cups cheddar cheese, shredded

Saute onion and bay leaf in butter or margarine; remove bay leaf. Mix together onion, rice, cottage cheese, sour cream, chiles and 1 1/2 cups cheese in large casserole dish. Cover and bake at 375 degrees for 25 minutes. Sprinkle remaining 1/2 cup cheese on top and bake, uncovered, 10 minutes more. This dish can be cooked in microwave by heating 5 minutes on HIGH, covered. Remove cover, sprinkle with remaining cheese and microwave 1 minute longer, until cheese melts.

"This is a favorite in my Foods Class and was the recipe given to me by my mother, who makes it for all the pot lucks she attends."

Jan Hirth   **Saddleback High School, Santa Ana, CA**

Spicy Black Beans
Serves 6

    1 pound black beans
    4 1/2 cups water
    1/4 pound bacon, chopped
    5 medium cloves garlic, minced
    2 stalks celery, minced
    1 large carrot, peeled, diced
    1 medium onion, diced
    1 jalapeño chili, seeded, minced
    1 bay leaf
    1 tablespoon chili powder
    1 teaspoon cumin
    1/2 to 1 teaspoon cayenne pepper
    1/2 to 3/4 teaspoon white pepper, freshly ground
    8 cups chicken broth
    Garnish: chopped red onion, sour cream, chopped chives

Soak beans in water 24 hours; drain and transfer to large saucepan. Cover with generous amount of cold water and bring to a boil; boil for 20 minutes. Drain and rinse beans; set aside. In large saucepan, cook bacon over medium heat until crisp. Mix in garlic, celery, carrot, onion, jalapeño and bay leaf. Cook until vegetables are tender, stirring occasionally, about 10 minutes. Add chili powder, cumin, cayenne and white pepper. Stir until aromatic, about 1 minute. Add beans and chicken broth. Cook at a slow boil until beans are tender and most of the liquid is absorbed, stirring occasionally, about 1 1/2 to 2 hours. Season to taste with salt, remove bay leaf; garnish as desired and serve.

"Serve with grilled pork loin and tomatillo sauce."

Vicki Giannetti   **Foothill High School, Sacramento, CA**

Spicy Potato Salad
Serves 6

    6 White Rose potatoes
    1 large green pepper, chopped
    2 medium tomatoes, diced
    1 small red onion, chopped
    1/4 cup cilantro, minced
    1 (2.5 ounce) can olives, sliced
    1 cup sour cream
    2/3 cup picante sauce
    1/2 cup jalapeños, sliced (optional)

In a large saucepan, simmer potatoes in water for 25 to 35 minutes; cool. In a large bowl, toss together green pepper, tomatoes and red onion. Add cilantro and olives to bowl and toss again. Dice the cooled potatoes, with skins still on, and add to vegetables in bowl. In a small bowl, combine sour cream and picante sauce. Pour over salad and toss. If desired, toss in jalapeños (they may be served separately) and chill for 3 hours or overnight to combine flavors.

Cathy Miller   **Montclair High School, Montclair, CA**

Super Beans
Serves 8

- 1 pound bulk pork sausage
- 3 cloves garlic, chopped
- 1 teaspoon cumin
- 1 tablespoon chili powder
- 1 (4 ounce) can green chiles, diced
- 2 (10 ounce) cans pinto beans in chili sauce

Saute sausage; drain fat. Stir in remaining ingredients and pour into a casserole dish. Bake at 350 degrees for 30 minutes.

"Add jalapeños for spicier flavor."

Edna O'Neal   **Durango High School, Las Vegas, NV**

Torta de Calabazas
Serves 6

- 2 pounds zucchini, washed, stems removed
- 1 onion, minced
- 1 clove garlic, minced
- 2 tablespoons oil
- 3 tomatoes, peeled, chopped
- 1 tablespoon parsley, minced
- 1/2 cup cheese, shredded
- salt and pepper
- 2 eggs, separated
- 2 tablespoons butter
- 2 tablespoons bread crumbs

Cook zucchini until tender in small amount of water; drain and chop. Fry onion and garlic in oil; add chopped tomato and parsley, then add zucchini and shredded cheese. Season to taste with salt and pepper. Beat egg whites until stiff but not dry. In another bowl, beat egg yolks, then add to whites and beat well. Butter a casserole and sprinkle with half of the bread crumbs. Pour in a layer of egg batter, then a layer of zucchini mixture. Repeat until all ingredients are used. Over top layer, sprinkle remaining bread crumbs, dot with butter and bake at 375 degrees until browned, about 15 to 20 minutes.

Linda Robinson   **Royal High School, Simi Valley, CA**

BEEF, LAMB & PORK

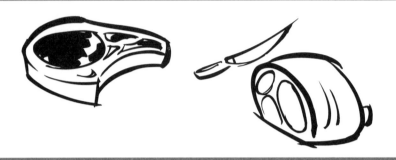

A Different Kind of Enchilada!

Serves 5

 1 pound hamburger
 $^1/_2$ onion, chopped
 1 to 2 teaspoons chili powder
 1 teaspoon tamale powder
 1 teaspoon paprika
 1 teaspoon salt
 1 teaspoon pepper
 3 tablespoons Ghiradelli chocolate, grated
 1 teaspoon cinnamon
 1 teaspoon cloves
 3 (8 ounce) cans tomato sauce
 3 cups water
 1 pound cheddar cheese, shredded
 12 flour tortillas

Brown hamburger with onion; drain excess fat. Add remaining ingredients (except cheese and tortillas) and cook until sauce becomes thick, about 20 minutes. Dip flour tortilla into sauce, place on plate, fill with shredded cheese, fold and top with sauce. Serve.

"This sauce is a bit sweeter than most.
A quick and easy recipe from my mom's kitchen."

Maria Fregulia   **Lassen Union High School, Susanville, CA**

Acapulco Casserole

Serves 4

1 pound ground beef
1 (15 ounce) can cream style corn
1 (15 ounce) can tomato sauce
1 (15 ounce) can kidney beans
1 cup celery, chopped
1 1/2 tablespoons worcestershire sauce
1 cup onion, chopped (optional)
1 teaspoon chili powder (optional)
1 clove garlic, pressed (optional)
6 corn tortillas
1/2 cup cheddar cheese, shredded

Brown ground beef in skillet; drain fat. Add corn, tomato sauce, beans, celery, worcestershire sauce and optional items, if using; cook 3 minutes. In round 2 quart casserole, layer 1 tortilla, 1 cup sauce; repeat until all ingredients are used. Sprinkle cheese on top and bake at 350 degrees for 30 minutes.

"This comes from the kitchen of Trevor H. Smith."

Becky Oppen   **Dana Hills High School, Dana Point, CA**

AJ's Alfonso-Style Carne Asada Marinade

vegetable oil
salt
black pepper
granulated or powdered garlic
oregano
ground cumin
jalapeño slices, with juice
lemon or lime juice
Condiments: chopped tomatoes, onion, shredded lettuce, cheese, sour cream,
    guacamole, sliced olives, salsa

You may use this marinade with any cut of meat. Season as follows: Cover each side of meat with oil. Season meat with salt, pepper (the more black pepper, the hotter the flavor), garlic, oregano, cumin and jalapeño. Layer seasoned meat flat in a sealable baster container, squeezing citrus juice over each layer. Store in refrigerator 12 to 24 hours, rotating container throughout the day. Do not store longer than four days. Grill both sides of meat quickly until done to your taste. Slice into thin, long strips and serve with desired condiments.

"My friend, A.J., brought this to our American Sewing Guild meeting.
We all enjoyed it!"

Luann Goedert   **Carlsbad High School, Carlsbad, CA**

Authentic Homemade Taco Meat & Seasoning

Serves 4

> 1 cup water
> 3 dried California chile pods
> 1 to 2 tomatoes, skin removed
> 1 pound ground beef or turkey
> 1 medium onion, diced
> 1 teaspoon onion powder
> 1 teaspoon oregano
> $1/2$ teaspoon cumin
> $1/2$ teaspoon pepper
> salt, to taste
> 2 tablespoons vinegar
> chopped potato or zucchini (optional)
> taco shells

In a saucepan, place water, dried chiles and tomatoes; bring to a boil, then simmer 5 to 10 minutes, until tender. Cool slightly and process in a blender or food processor; set aside. In a skillet, brown ground meat and onion together; drain fat. Add onion powder, oregano, cumin, pepper, salt and vinegar. (If using potato or zucchini, add to meat and cook until tender.) Add chile sauce to mixture and heat thoroughly. Serve with soft or crisp taco shells.

"Thanks to my friend, Anna Tapia, who shared this recipe. It is so much better than taco seasoning from a package and not much more work. Try it!!"

Ruth Anne Mills   **Los Alisos Intermediate School, Mission Viejo, CA**

Awesome Tortilla Bake

Serves 8

> 1 $1/2$ pounds lean ground beef
> 1 large onion, chopped
> 1 (14.5 ounce) can Mexican-style stewed tomatoes, undrained
> 1 (10 ounce) can mild enchilada sauce
> 8 ounces processed cheese, sliced
> 2 teaspoons ground cumin
> $1/2$ teaspoon salt
> $1/2$ teaspoon pepper
> 2 cups tortilla chips, crushed
> 1 (3 ounce) package cream cheese, softened
> 8 (8") flour tortillas
> 1 (4 ounce) can green chiles, diced
> 1 cup jack cheese, shredded

Brown ground beef and onion a large skillet, stirring until meat crumbles; drain fat. Stir in tomatoes, enchilada sauce, sliced cheese, cumin, salt and pepper. Cook over low heat, stirring constantly, until cheese melts; set aside. Preheat oven to 350 degrees. Place crushed tortilla chips in greased 9" x 13" baking dish. Spoon $2/3$ beef mixture over tortilla chips. Spread about 1 teaspoon cream cheese evenly on 1 side of each tortillas and sprinkle evenly with chiles. Fold tortillas in half and arrange on beef mixture. Spoon remaining beef mixture on top of tortillas and cover. Bake 20 minutes. Uncover casserole and sprinkle with jack cheese. Bake 5 minutes more to melt cheese.

"A family favorite. Easy–quick and tasty!"

Cari Sheridan   **Grace Yokley School, Ontario, CA**

Baja Pizza Pouch

Serves 10

> Photo Opposite
> **Page 97**

   1 1/4 pound chorizo pork
   3/4 pound ground beef
   1 (48 ounce) can Rosarita Spicy Refried Beans
   3/4 teaspoon garlic powder
   3/4 teaspoon ground cumin
   1 (15 ounce) can Angela Mia Crushed Tomatoes
   2 1/2 tablespoons dried oregano
   2 1/2 pounds pizza dough
   5 ounces Wisconsin Monterey Jack cheese, shredded
   1/3 cup Wesson oil

Saute chorizo and ground beef. Add beans, garlic powder and cumin to meat mixture; simmer about 15 minutes. In separate pan, simmer tomatoes and oregano for 15 minutes. Cut dough into 4 ounce portions. On floured surface, roll out dough portions into 6" circles, 1/4" thick. To assemble each calzone: Place dough circles on lightly oiled baking sheet. Spread 1/4 cup refried beans mixture on half the dough circle, to within 1/4" from edge. Spoon 2 tablespoons tomato sauce on top of refried beans mixture. Sprinkle 1/2 cup shredded Monterey Jack cheese on top of sauce. Fold circles in half and moisten edges with water. Press edges firmly together with a fork. Brush calzone lightly with oil. Bake at 400 degrees for 15 minutes, until golden brown. Serve with a side of Calavo Western Style guacamole.

Wisconsin Milk Marketing Board   **Madison, WI**

Beef Chilaquiles

Serves 6

   1 package corn tortillas
   1 cup oil
   1 cup El Patio hot chile sauce
   1 cup enchilada sauce
   1 pound ground beef
   salt and pepper, to taste
   1 small can black olives, sliced
   1/4 pound mild cheddar cheese, shredded
   1/4 pound jack cheese, shredded

Cut tortillas into triangles and fry until crisp; drain and lightly salt. Place chile sauce and enchilada sauce in pan; simmer on low heat. In another pan, brown ground beef, season with salt and pepper; drain fat. Add tortillas to simmering sauce, stirring to coat. Layer tortillas in large baking pan, covering bottom. Top with a layer of meat, olives and cheese; repeat. Sprinkle cheese and olives on top and bake at 350 degrees for 5 minutes, until cheese melts.

"This is like an enchilada casserole."

Janie Greaves   **Central High School, Fresno, CA**

Beef Enchiladas

Serves 4

    1 package enchilada sauce mix
    1 (6 ounce) can tomato paste
    3 cups water
    2 cups chopped or ground beef
    16 ounces Monterey Jack or cheddar cheese, shredded
    8 corn tortillas
    1/4 cup olives, chopped
    1/3 cup salsa

Combine sauce mix with tomato paste and water in saucepan; bring to a boil, then reduce heat and simmer, uncovered 15 minutes, stirring constantly. Brown beef thoroughly until crumbly; drain fat; cool. Mix 1 1/2 cups shredded cheese into meat. Pour 1 cup enchilada sauce into baking pan. Make enchiladas one at a time by dipping 1 corn tortilla into sauce. Place 1/2 cup meat and cheese mixture in center of each tortilla. Add olives and 1 teaspoon sauce down center. Roll up and place seam side down in baking dish. Repeat. Pour remaining sauce over enchiladas and top with remaining cheese and salsa. Bake at 350 degrees for 20 minutes. Serve hot.

"Yummy!"

Alice Claiborne   **Fairfield High School, Fairfield, CA**

Beef Taquitos

Serves 6

    1 (12 ounce) can roast beef with gravy
    prime rib seasoning (available from most butcher counters)
    12 corn tortillas
    oil, for frying
    prepared guacamole, for serving

Drain gravy from roast beef and set aside for another recipe. Divide beef into 12 equal portions. Sprinkle each portion with a little seasoning. Soften corn tortillas over gas flame or lightly fry in hot oil for a few seconds; drain on paper towels. Place one portion of roast beef down the center of each tortilla. Roll up and stack, seam side down (to keep from unrolling) until ready to fry. (Taquitos may be covered and refrigerated or frozen at this point.) When ready to fry, heat about 1/4" to 1/2" oil in skillet, over medium-high heat. Using tongs, place in hot oil and fry until golden brown and crisp. (If taquitos are frozen, use lower heat, as they will spatter when placed in oil.) Remove from pan and drain on paper towels. Serve with guacamole.

Carol Goddard   **Alhambra High School, Alhambra, CA**

Big Burrito Party

Serves 8

    1 (12" wide) board of desired length (6 to 8 feet), covered with
        heavy duty aluminum foil
    1 (12") package flour tortillas heated
    1 large can refried beans, heated
    2 to 2 1/2 pounds ground beef, seasoned to your taste
    1 1/2 pounds cheddar cheese, grated
    6 to 8 green onions, finely chopped
    4 medium tomatoes, chopped
    1 to 2 cups salsa
    1 (32 ounce) carton sour cream, stirred
    1 cup prepared guacamole
    1 can black olives, pitted, chopped

Place foil covered board on table top or between two card tables (if very long). Wrap tortillas in slightly damp clean kitchen towel then aluminum foil. Heat in a 300 degree over for 20 minutes or until warm. Chop or prepare all food products and place in bowls when ready to assemble.

Each guest should have something to do to assemble the burrito. Be sure to give explicit directions to each person. Everything should be ready before you begin! Place tortillas on foil overlapping about one third. Quickly spread a 3" wide strip of hot refried beans, then top with meat, half of the cheese, green onions, tomatoes, salsa, remaining cheese and sour cream. Roll up tortillas (first one side, then the other) placing seam side down. Pat down gently to hold all together. (Everyone needs to help with this step!) Quickly top with guacamole and chopped olives. Cut into serving sizes and enjoy!

"This is a recipe that some of you have possibly used, but some of you have asked me for it! It's a great fun activity for FHA week. Have students sign up for what ingredients he or she can bring, then fill in the gaps!"

Cheryle Apple   **Rio Vista High School, Rio Vista, CA**

Burrito Pie

Serves 6

    1/4 cup salad oil
    4 (8") flour tortillas
    1/2 pound ground beef
    1 medium onion, diced
    1 small clove garlic, minced
    1 (4ounce) can green chiles, diced, drained
    1 (8 ounce) can refried beans
    1/3 cup hot taco sauce
    1/2 pound Monterey Jack cheese, shredded
    Garnish: 1 cup shredded lettuce, 1 diced tomato, 5 large ripe olives, sliced

Heat oil in a 10" skillet over medium heat; fry tortillas, one at a time, until lightly browned and blistered, about 30 seconds each side. With tongs remove tortillas to paper towels to drain. Discard remaining oil. Preheat oven to 350 degrees. In same skillet, over high heat, cook ground beef with onion and garlic until well browned, stirring occasionally. Remove skillet from heat; stir in green chiles, refried beans and taco sauce. In 9" pie plate, place 1 tortilla, top with one fourth bean/meat mixture and one fourth of cheese. Repeat three times. Bake 30 minutes until heated through. To serve, sprinkle with lettuce, tomatoes and olives.

Judi Topp   **A.B. Miller High School, Fontana, CA**

Caballero Casserole

Serves 10

    2 (15 ounce) cans Hormel Tamales
    2 (12 ounce) cans whole kernel corn with sweet peppers, undrained
    1 (14 1/2 ounce) can pizza sauce
    Cheese Olive Topping:
    1/2 cup all-purpose flour
    3/4 cup corn meal
    1 packet cheese sauce mix
    1 1/2 teaspoons baking powder
    1 teaspoon salt
    1 egg
    3/4 cup milk
    1/4 cup oil
    2 tablespoons ripe olives, chopped

Cut each tamale into 6 pieces. Place half tamales in bottom of 13"x 9" pan; spread with 1 can corn. Top with remaining tamales and other can of corn. Pour pizza sauce over top. In large mixing bowl, combine dry ingredients for Cheese Olive Topping. Add remaining ingredients and stir until a dough forms. Spread dough over top of casserole. Bake at 375 degrees for 30 to 35 minutes.

Astrid Curfman   **Newcomb Academy, Long Beach, CA**

Calabacitas (Steak and Zucchini)

Serves 8

    1/4 cup butter or margarine
    2 pounds lean sirloin, cut into 1" cubes
    5 medium-sized zucchini, thinly sliced
    2 cups whole kernel corn, drained
    1 (4 ounce) can green chiles, diced
    2 cloves garlic, minced
    1 teaspoon salt
    dash Mexican oregano
    1/4 teaspoon cumin
    3/4 cup cheddar cheese, shredded (optional)

Melt butter in large skillet. Brown steak cubes, a few at a time, removing pieces to a bowl as they brown. Saute zucchini until slightly tender, about 10 minutes. Return meat to skillet. Add corn, chiles, garlic, salt, oregano and cumin. Cook, stirring occasionally, until meat is tender, about 10 minutes. Add cheese, stir until melted.

"Pam Bartlett shared this family recipe with my classes. It was a hit!"

Cindy Peters   **Deer Valley High School, Antioch, CA**

California Tamale Pie

Serves 8

    1 pound lean ground beef
    3/4 cup yellow cornmeal
    1 1/2 cups milk
    1 egg, beaten
    1 package chili seasoning mix
    1 tablespoon seasoned salt
    1 (16 ounce) can tomatoes, cut up
    1 (16 ounce) can whole kernel corn, drained
    1 (2.25 ounce) can ripe olives, drained, sliced
    1 cup cheddar cheese, shredded

In skillet, cook meat until crumbly; drain. In large bowl, mix cornmeal, milk and egg. Add drained meat, chili seasoning, seasoned salt, tomatoes, corn and olives; mix well. Pour into casserole dish or crock pot. If baking in oven, cover casserole and bake at 350 degrees for 40 minutes or until bubbly. Top with cheese and return to oven until cheese is melted. If using crockpot, cover and cook on high 2 to 3 hours or on low heat 5 to 6 hours. Top with cheese, then cover until cheese has melted.

"This recipe is easy and a good mix of flavors."

Dale Sheehan　　　　　　　　　　　　　　**Santana High School, Santee, CA**

Chile Colorado

Serves 4

    3 cups beef or pork, cut into cubes
    3 tablespoons oil
    2 tablespoons flour
    3 teaspoons chili powder
    1 large onion, chopped
    1 clove garlic, crushed
    1/4 teaspoon ground cumin
    3 cups water
    1 bay leaf
    salt and pepper, to taste

In a large pot, brown meat in oil. Add flour and stir until browned. Add next four ingredients and cook until onion is tender. Slowly add water and bring to a boil. Reduce heat, add bay leaf and simmer until meat is tender, 2 to 3 hours. Salt and pepper, to taste.

"This recipe can also be used as a filling for burritos."

Bonnie Shrock　　　　　　　　　　　　**Kearny High School, San Diego, CA**

Chile Verde

Serves 4

    1 onion, chopped
    1 clove garlic, minced
    1 tablespoon olive oil
    2 pounds pork roast, cut into 1" cubes
    2 (7.75 ounce) cans El Patio tomato sauce
    1 (8 ounce) jar Embasa Jalapeño Green Salsa
    1 (4 ounce) can green chiles, diced
    1 to 2 tablespoons cornstarch, dissolved in 1/4 cup water
    12 flour tortillas

Saute onion and garlic in olive oil. Add pork cubes and brown lightly. Add tomato sauce, green salsa and chiles; simmer 2 to 3 hours. Just before serving, stir in cornstarch dissolved in water to thicken sauce. Serve with warmed tortillas.

"I received this recipe from a student. I like to use the crockpot and have dinner practically ready when I come home from work."

Anne Silveira   **Shasta High School, Redding, CA**

Chile Verde Filling

Serves 4 - 6

    1 pound ground beef or leftover pork roast or turkey
    1 teaspoon salt
    1 clove garlic or 1/8 teaspoon garlic powder
    1 can green chiles, diced
    1 to 3 jalapeño peppers, diced
    6 to 8 tablespoons flour
    2 to 3 cups water

Brown hamburger, salt and garlic until no longer pink; drain fat. Stir in chiles. Mix together flour and water and stir into meat mixture. Simmer 5 to 10 minutes, until sauce has thickened to desired consistency.

Note: This can be used to stuff enchiladas, eat on pinto beans, eggs or fried potatoes (like bread and gravy Mexican-style!) or rolled up in a tortilla for a chile verde burrito.

"Hot or mild, depending on how many jalapeños are used."

Sue Fullmer   **Cimarron-Memorial High School, Las Vegas, NV**

Chili Burrito Cups

Serves 8

    2 1/2 pound boneless beef chuck pot roast
    1 medium onion, sliced
    1/2 teaspoon salt
    1/4 teaspoon pepper
    water
    1 large onion, chopped

Photo Opposite
Page 129

1 tablespoon vegetable oil
1 (16 ounce) can pinto, kidney or pink beans, drained
1 (14.5 to 16 ounce) can tomatoes
1 (6 ounce) can tomato paste
1 (4 ounce) can green chiles, diced
1 tablespoon chili powder
8 (7 to 8") flour tortillas
Garnish: sour cream, guacamole

Cut boneless beef chuck pot roast into 3 to 4 pieces. Place beef, sliced onion, salt and pepper in Dutch oven. Add water up to 1/2" of pan; cover tightly and cook slowly on top of range or in 300 degree oven for 2 to 2 1/2 hours or until beef is tender. Cool slightly in juices. Pour off juices; skim off fat and reserve 1 cup juices. Separate beef with the grain into thin shreds using two forks; reserve. In same Dutch oven, saute chopped onion in oil until tender. Add reserved shredded beef and 1 cup juices, beans, tomatoes, tomato paste, chiles and chili powder. Bring to a boil; reduce heat and simmer 1 hour or until thickened, stirring occasionally. Meanwhile prepare tortilla cups. Gently press 4 flour tortillas into four 10 ounce custard cups. Microwave on HIGH 2 minutes, Rotate and rearrange custard cups; continue cooking at HIGH 1 to 2 minutes. Carefully lift tortillas out and cool on wire rack. Repeat procedure to make 8 tortilla cups. Spoon an equal amount of beef mixture into each tortilla cup. Serve with desired garnish.

National Cattleman's Beef Association　　　　　　**Chicago, IL**

Chorizo With Eggs

Serves 2

2 chorizo sausages
2 tablespoons onion, chopped
4 eggs, beaten

In heavy skillet, mash and cook sausage; drain excess fat. Add onion and cook until limp. Add beaten eggs and stir as eggs begin to set. Cook to desired firmness. Serve at once with tortillas.

"Breakfast with a Mexican flavor!"

Kathy Warren　　　　**C.K. McClatchy High School, Sacramento, CA**

Cowboy Beef Pizzas

Serves 4

1/2 pound ground beef
1/2 teaspoon salt
1 (8 ounce) can refrigerated biscuits
1/2 cup pizza sauce
1/2 cup mozzarella cheese, shredded
1 small can black olives, drained
1 (2.5 ounce) can mushrooms, sliced, drained
1/4 cup bell pepper, chopped

Lightly brown ground beef in skillet until all pinkness is gone; drain off fat. Season with salt. Roll biscuits out on a lightly floured board into circles 4" to 5" in diameter.

Place on baking sheet. Spread about 1 tablespoon pizza sauce on each biscuit circle. Top with ground beef and shredded cheese. Place olives, mushrooms and bell pepper on top. Bake at 400 degrees for 10 to 12 minutes.

Patty Stroming   **Mitchell Sr. Elementary, Atwater, CA**

Crepes Ensenada

Serves 6

Crepes:
12 thin slices ham
12 flour tortillas
1 pound jack cheese, cut into $1/2$" sticks
1 can green chiles, whole, cut into $1/4$" strips
paprika
Cheese Sauce:
$1/4$ pound butter
$1/2$ cup flour
1 quart milk
$3/4$ pound cheddar cheese, shredded
$1/2$ teaspoon ground mustard
$1/2$ teaspoon salt
dash pepper

Place one slice ham on each tortilla. Put 1 stick cheese in center of ham slice and top with strip of chile. Roll tortilla and secure with wood pick. Place rolled tortillas slightly separated in a greased 9" x 13" baking pan. Prepare cheese sauce: melt butter and blend in flour. Add milk, shredded cheese, mustard, salt and pepper. Cook, stirring constantly until smooth. Pour cheese sauce over crepes, sprinkle with paprika. Bake at 350 degrees for 45 minutes.

*"A family favorite, especially for special occasions.
My bunco group loves this recipe."*

Karen Frontino   **Arcadia High School, Arcadia, CA**

Crock Pot Tacos

Serves 8

2 medium tomatoes, peeled and chopped
1 Anaheim chile chopped
1 medium onion, chopped
2 to 3 cloves garlic, minced
1 flank steak
2 teaspoons chili powder
$1/2$ teaspoon ground cumin
$1/2$ teaspoon salt
$1/4$ teaspoon paprika
$1/4$ teaspoon oregano
$1/4$ cup water
taco shells
Garnish: shredded lettuce, chopped tomatoes, shredded cheese, taco sauce or salsa

Prepare vegetables and place in bottom of crock pot. Cut steak to fit and lay over vegetables. Mix seasonings together and sprinkle over meat. Add water. Cover and cook on high 3 to 4 hours OR begin cooking on high temperature for 1 hour, then change to low and cook for 8 to 12 hours. Remove meat from crock pot to cool, then shred and use in tacos. Serve in taco shells with desired garnishes.

"It's nice to come home from work with dinner almost ready."

Ellen Gordon   **Colton High School, Colton, CA**

Easy Chili & Corn Chip Casserole

Serves 6

> 1 (24 ounce) bag corn chips
> 1 (15 ounce) can chili
> 1 cup cheddar cheese, shredded
> 1 (15 ounce) can hominy
> 1 medium onion, chopped

Arrange ingredients in layers in casserole, ending with a generous topping of corn chips. Bake at 350 degrees for 30 minutes. Serve with corn chips.

"A delicious quick and easy recipe!"

Peg DellaZoppa   **Yucca Valley High School, Yucca Valley, CA**

Easy Taco Pizza

Serves 6

> 1 pound ground beef
> 1/2 cup onion, chopped
> 1 (2.5 ounce) can olives, sliced, drained
> 1 (8 ounce) can tomato sauce
> 1 (1.25 ounce) package taco seasoning mix
> 1 (10 ounce) can Pillsbury Refrigerated All Ready Pizza Crust
> 1 cup cheddar cheese, shredded
> *Garnish:* shredded lettuce, chopped tomatoes, sour cream, avocado slices

Heat oven to 425 degrees. In a large skillet, brown ground beef and onion; drain excess fat. Stir in olives, tomato sauce and taco seasoning. Prepare crust according to package directions using a 12" pizza pan or a 13" x 9" pan. Spread ground beef mixture over crust; sprinkle with cheese. Bake for 15 to 20 minutes, or until crust is golden brown. Garnish with desired garnishes.

"A fast, delicious meal when your schedule is cramped for time!"

Laurie Bleecker   **Centennial High School, Corona, CA**

Enchilada Casserole

Serves 6

1 1/2 pounds ground beef
1 large onion, chopped
garlic salt and pepper, to taste
1 (4 ounce) can green chiles, diced
2 small cans olives; chopped
1 can cream of mushroom soup
1 can cream of chicken soup
1 large can enchilada sauce
12 flour tortillas
4 cups cheddar cheese, shredded

Brown ground beef with onion and season to taste with garlic salt and pepper; drain excess fat. Add chiles, olives, soups and enchilada sauce; simmer 15 minutes. Cut up tortillas into bite-size pieces. In large casserole dish, layer tortillas, meat mixture and cheese, until all ingredients are used. Bake at 350 degrees until bubbly, approximately 30 minutes.

"This is my mother-in-law's recipe, and it has become a family favorite!"

LaRae Harguess **Hesperia High School, Hesperia, CA**

Evelyn's Chili Verde

Serves 4 - 6

2 pounds pork, cubed
2 (7 ounce) cans green chiles, whole
1 medium onion, chopped
1 (14 to 15 ounce) can tomatoes, diced
2 cloves garlic, minced
3/4 cup water
1 tablespoon cornstarch (optional)
salt

Brown meat in large pot using nonstick cooking spray or small amount of oil. Cut chiles into large chunks. Layer chiles, onion and tomatoes over meat. Sprinkle garlic over tomatoes. Pour water over mixture. Bring to a boil, then reduce heat and simmer 2 hours; do not stir. Check occasionally, adding water if necessary. Just before serving, dissolve cornstarch in 3 tablespoons water and stir into liquid in pan to thicken, if desired. Salt to taste.

"A family favorite from my mother-in-law. We eat it served over cooked pinto beans. Warmed flour tortillas and a green salad rounds out the meal."

Karen Lopez **San Luis Obispo High School, San Luis Obispo, CA**

Fiesta Party Steak

Serves 6

    1/2 cup flour
    1 teaspoon salt
    2 pounds round steak, cut in serving size pieces
    3 tablespoons oil
    1 large clove garlic, minced
    1 cup onion
    1 (4 ounce) can mushrooms, including liquid
    1 teaspoon ground cumin
    1 teaspoon chili powder
    1 (2.5 pound) can tomatoes, cut up, including juice
    1 teaspoon salt
    1 (4 ounce) can green chiles, diced
    pepper, to taste
    1 1/2 cups teleme or jack cheese, shredded

Combine flour and salt; dredge steak in flour mixture and brown in 1 tablespoon oil over medium-high heat. Transfer to a large flat casserole baking dish. Add remaining oil to skillet and saute garlic and onion for 2 to 3 minutes. Add remaining ingredients except cheese and simmer about 45 minutes, or until thickened. Taste and correct seasonings if necessary. Pour over browned steak pieces. Cover with foil and bake at 325 degrees for 1 hour, 45 minutes. Sprinkle with cheese and bake 15 minutes more, uncovered. Note: If desired, assemble steak day before and refrigerate before baking, add 20 minutes to baking time.

"Good with refried beans, green salad and tortilla chips or hot flour tortillas!"
Linda Brayton   **Grace Davis High School, Modesto, CA**

Green Chili

Serves 4

    1 pound beef stew meat, diced
    1 cup water
    1 clove garlic, minced
    1 teaspoon salt
    1 or 2 fresh hot green chile peppers
    2 green bell peppers, diced

In 2 quart saucepan, combine beef, water, garlic and salt; cover and simmer 1 hour. Meanwhile, place chile peppers on baking sheet; bake in 400 degree oven until peppers are browned and skin splits, about 25 minutes. Cool slightly. While still warm, peel skin, halve peppers and remove seeds. Finely chop chile peppers and add to meat mixture along with bell peppers. Simmer, covered, 20 minutes. Uncover and simmer 20 minutes more.

"Good as a side dish, in burritos or by itself with warmed flour tortillas."
Joanne Montoy   **Esperanza High School, Anaheim, CA**

"Hits The Spot" Mexican Casserole

Serves 6

2 cups macaroni, cooked
1 can chili con carne, with beans
2 cans tomato sauce
3 small green Torrido chili peppers, diced
1/4 teaspoon salt
1/4 teaspoon Tabasco sauce
2 cans Vienna sausages, diced
1/4 cup Parmesan cheese, grated

Mix together cooked macaroni, chili con carne and tomato sauce. Add chopped peppers, salt, Tabasco sauce and Vienna sausages. Place in casserole dish. Sprinkle with cheese. Bake at 325 degrees for 20 minutes or until casserole bubbles.

"I made this recipe when I was a starving college student!"

Mary Springhorn   **Anderson High School, Anderson, CA**

Marilyn's Tacos

Serves 6

1 pound ground beef or turkey
1 onion, chopped
1 teaspoon salt
1/2 teaspoon leaf oregano
1 (16 ounce) can tomatoes
1 (8 ounce) can tomato sauce
Garnish: shredded cheese, lettuce, tomatoes, onion, olives, sour cream, hot sauce

In a large frying pan or electric skillet, brown meat with onion, salt and oregano until meat is no longer pink; drain off excess fat. Add tomatoes and tomato suace. Cover and simmer about 1 hour. Serve in taco shells, or on top of corn chips with desired garnishes.

"A regular growing up. Passed from my grandmother, my mother then to me."

Teresa Hayes   **Buena High School, Ventura, CA**

Meatballs Con Queso

Serves 6

1 1/2 pounds ground beef
2 eggs
1/2 cup milk
1/2 cup bread crumbs
1/2 onion, sauteed
2 pounds Velveeta, cubed
1 package taco seasoning
1 (4 ounce) can green chiles, diced
3 cups rice, cooked

In a large bowl, mix together ground beef, eggs, milk, bread crumbs and onion. Form into meatballs and fry in skillet or bake in oven at 350 degrees for 30 minutes. In a large skillet, melt Velveeta with taco seasoning and chiles. Add meatballs, stirring gently until heated through. Serve atop rice.

"This is always a big hit. Delicious!"

Debbie Powers   **Griffiths Middle School, Downey, CA**

Meaty Beef Taquitos

Makes 36

1 (3 1/2 to 4 pound) boneless chuck roast
3/4 teaspoon garlic salt
1/4 teaspoon pepper
3 to 4 cloves garlic, minced
36 corn tortillas
1 cup oil, for frying
Garnish: shredded lettuce, guacamole

Season meat with garlic salt, pepper and minced garlic. Wrap roast tightly in heavy duty aluminum foil and roast at 350 degrees for 3 hours, until fork tender. Remove roast from foil, reserving juices and set aside. While meat is still hot, shred with a fork. Strain fat from meat juices and pour 1/2 cup meat juices back over meat; toss and let cool. In a small 8" fry pan, warm corn tortillas, one at a time until soft and pliable. Fill each tortilla with 3 tablespoons shredded meat and roll tightly; secure with toothpick. Place taquitos in ziploc bag to keep tortillas from drying out as you make them. (At this point, you may freeze taquitos for later use.) To serve, heat 1" oil in a pan and fry taquitos until crispy. (If taquitos are frozen, be careful when frying as oil will spatter from ice crystals.) Drain on paper towels and serve on a bed of shredded lettuce with guacamole on top.

*"Easy to do ahead–freeze and fry last minute for parties, as main dish,
or cut in half and serve as appetizers."*

Linda Hsieh   **Rowland High School, Rowland Heights, CA**

Mexi-Cheese Burgers

Serves 8

1 egg
1/4 cup taco sauce
3/4 cup dry bread crumbs
1 (4 ounce) can green chiles, diced
1/2 teaspoon salt
1 1/2 pounds ground beef
8 slices American cheese
8 hamburger buns

In a mixing bowl, combine egg, taco sauce, bread crumbs, green chiles and salt. Add ground beef; mix thoroughly. Shape beef mixture into eight patties. Grill over coals for 8 to 10 minutes. Turn and grill until desired doneness. Add one slice cheese to each patty and cook until cheese melts. Serve on buns.

"A tasty change from the traditional cheeseburger."

Joanne Fial   **East Middle School, Downey, CA**

Mexi-Lamb Tortilla Lasagna

Serves 4 - 6

Photo Opposite
Page 96

12 ounces lean ground American lamb
1 cup salsa
1 (8 ounce) can red kidney beans, drained
1 (8 ounce) carton light sour cream
$1/4$ cup green chiles, diced (about $1/2$ of a 4 ounce can)
$1/4$ cup cheddar cheese, shredded
1 tablespoon flour
nonstick cooking spray
3 (10") flour tortillas
1 cup lettuce, shredded
$1/4$ cup tomato, chopped
Garnish: shredded cheese, salsa

In large saucepan, cook ground lamb until no pink remains. Remove from heat; drain well. Stir in 1 cup salsa and drained beans; set aside. In a bowl, mix sour cream, chiles, $1/4$ cup cheese and flour. Spray a 10" pie plate or quiche dish with nonstick cooking spray. Place one tortilla in pie plate or quiche dish. Top with $3/4$ cup of meat mixture and $1/2$ of sour cream mixture. Top with a second tortilla and repeat with $3/4$ cup meat and remaining sour cream. Top with a third tortilla and remaining meat. Bake at 350 degrees for 25 minutes or until heated through. Let stand 5 minutes before cutting into wedges to serve. Top each serving with shredded lettuce and chopped tomato. Garnish as desired.

American Sheep Industry   **Englewood, CO**

Mexicali Pizza Wheel

Makes 1

Mexicali filling:
1 pound ground beef
1 (8.75 ounce) can kidney beans, drained
1 (8 ounce) can tomato sauce
2 teaspoons chili powder
1 (4 ounce) jar pimentos, diced, drained
1 cup cheese, shredded
2 tablespoons mild green chiles, diced
Pizza dough:
2 $3/4$ cups all-purpose flour
$1/2$ cup cornmeal
1 package Fleischmann's Rapid Rise Yeast
1 tablespoon sugar
1 teaspoon salt
1 cup very warm water (125 to 130 degrees)
2 tablespoons margarine, softened

Brown ground beef; drain excess fat. Add kidney beans, tomato sauce and chili powder. Cook, stirring occasionally, until dry; cool. Stir in pimentos, shredded cheese and green chiles; set aside. Make dough: Combine 1 cup flour, cornmeal, undissolved yeast, sugar and salt. Stir water and margarine into dry ingredients. Stir in enough remaining flour to make soft dough. Knead on lightly floured surface until smooth and elastic, about 4 to 6 minutes. Cover; let rest 10 minutes. Roll dough to 15" circle. Place in greased 14" pizza pan, forming a standing rim of dough around edge. Cut a 7" X in center of circle, Cut another X to form 8 pie shaped wedges in center. Spread a 3" border of Mexicali filling evenly around edge of dough. Pull cut points of dough over filling; tuck under rim and press to seal. Bake at 425 degrees on lowest oven rack for 20 minutes or until done. Garnish as desired.

"Students and Super Bowl fans love this recipe."

Jill Burnham   **Bloomington High School, Bloomington, CA**

Mexican Lasagna

Serves 12

> 1 1/2 pounds ground beef
> 1 teaspoon seasoned salt
> 1 package taco seasoning mix
> 1 cup tomatoes, diced
> 1 (16 ounce) can tomato sauce
> 1 (4 ounce) can green chiles, diced
> 8 ounces ricotta cheese
> 2 eggs
> 9 corn tortillas
> 10 ounces Monterey Jack cheese, shredded

In large skillet, brown ground beef; drain fat. Add seasoned salt, taco mix, tomatoes, tomato sauce and chiles; blend well. Bring to a boil; reduce heat and simmer, uncovered, 10 minutes. In small bowl, combine ricotta cheese and eggs. In bottom of 13" x 9" pan, spread 1/2 meat mixture. Top with 1/2 tortillas; spread 1/2 of ricotta cheese and egg mixture over tortillas and top with 1/2 shredded cheese. Repeat once more, ending with shredded cheese. Bake, uncovered, at 350 degrees for 25 to 30 minutes. Let stand 10 minutes before cutting into squares to serve.

"This can be made ahead and refrigerated; add 10 to 15 minutes to baking time or freeze, and defrost, before baking."

Vicki Pearl   **Giano Intermediate School, La Puente, CA**

Mexican Lasagna With Noodles

Serves 6

> 1 (1.75 ounce) package Chili-O Mix
> 1 pound ground beef
> 1 tablespoon oil
> 1 (1 pound) can tomatoes
> 1 (1 pound) can kidney beans
> 1/2 cup water
> 1 pound lasagna noodles
> 2 cups cottage cheese
> 1 1/2 cups cheddar cheese, shredded

Prepare Chili-O according to package directions using beef, oil, tomatoes, beans and water. Cook lasagna noodles according to package directions. In shallow 3 quart baking pan, alternate layers of noodles, meat sauce, cottage cheese and shredded cheese, making 3 layers, ending with sauce and shredded cheese. Bake at 350 degrees for 30 minutes. Let stand 15 minutes to set before cutting to serve.

Pam Fecchino   **Cimarron-Memorial High School, Las Vegas, NV**

Mexican Lasagna With Tortillas
Serves 6

    1 pound lean ground beef
    1 medium onion, chopped
    1 clove garlic, finely minced
    2 (8 ounce) cans tomato sauce
    1 1/2 cups water
    1 to 2 tablespoons chili powder
    1/4 teaspoon salt
    9 tortillas
    1/2 cup sour cream
    2 cups Monterey Jack or cheddar cheese, shredded
    1/2 cup olives, chopped (optional)

Brown meat with onion and garlic in skillet; drain fat. Add tomato sauce, water, chili powder and salt; simmer 20 minutes. In a 13" x 9" pan, spoon 1/4 of mixture on bottom. Arrange 3 tortillas over meat sauce, overlapping if necessary. Spread 1/3 of sour cream over tortillas. Sprinkle with 1/3 of cheese. Repeat. Garnish with olives and bake at 350 degrees for 20 minutes, until hot and bubbly.

Pamela Campion   **Dublin High School, Dublin, CA**

Mexican Pizza
Makes 3

    1/2 pound ground beef
    1 1/3 cups salsa, divided
    2 cups refried beans
    6 flour tortillas
    2 cups jack and cheddar cheese, combined, shredded
    1/5 green pepper, chopped
    2 green onions, finely chopped
    1/3 cup black olives, sliced

Cook ground beef until no longer pink; drain fat and discard. Mix 1/3 cup salsa with meat and set aside. Heat beans in microwave, about 1 minute. To assemble each pizza, place tortilla on jelly roll pan. Spread with refried beans and top with meat. Place another tortilla on top of meat spread with 1/2 cup salsa; top with cheese and vegetables. Repeat, making two more pizzas. Cover with Saran wrap and refrigerate. To bake, preheat oven to 400 degrees. Unwrap pizzas and bake 10 minutes. Slice with pizza cutter to serve.

"A favorite of my foods classes!"

Janis M. Brokaw   **Mountain Shadows Middle School, Rohnert Park, CA**

Mexican Quiche
Serves 6 - 8

1 (9") unbaked pie shell
1 1/2 pounds ground beef
1/2 onion, chopped
1/2 to 1 (4 ounce) can green chiles, diced
1 1/2 cups Monterey Jack cheese, shredded
1 cup half & half
2 tablespoons flour
2 eggs

Brown ground beef with onion; drain fat; add chiles. Sprinkle a layer of cheese on bottom of pie shell. Top with a layer of meat. Repeat layers. Beat together half & half, eggs and flour. Pour over layers. Bake at 400 degrees for 40 to 45 minutes. Let stand 10 minutes before serving.

Marion S. Anderson   **A.G. Currie Middle School, Tustin, CA**

Navajo Tacos
Makes 3

Chili Beans:
1 cup Great Northern or Pinto beans
1 quart water
1 large onion, chopped
1 tablespoon salad oil
1 pound ground beef or bulk pork sausage
3 cups chicken broth
1 tablespoon chili powder
2 cloves garlic , minced
2 teaspoons ground cumin
2 teaspoons dried oregano
2 teaspoons dried basil
Fry Bread:
2 cups all-purpose flour
1/2 cup instant nonfat dry milk
1 tablespoon baking powder
1/2 teaspoon salt
2 tablespoons shortening
3/4 cup water
2 cups oil, for frying
Tacos:
2 to 3 firm ripe tomatoes, cored
3/4 pound mild cheddar, cheese, shredded
1head iceberg lettuce, finely shredded
1 1/4 cups green onions, thinly sliced
1 cup salsa
1 cup sour cream

Chili Beans: Place beans in a 4 quart pan with water; bring to a boil. Cook, uncovered 10 minutes. Remove from heat, cover and let stand 1 hour. Drain beans and set aside. Rinse and dry pan, return to medium heat. Add onion and oil; stirring until onion is limp, 3 to 4 minutes. Add onion to beans. Crumble ground beef into pan, cooking over high heat until well browned; drain fat. Add beans and onion to meat. Stir in chicken broth, chili powder, garlic, cumin, oregano and basil. Bring to a boil over high heat; simmer, covered until beans are tender to bite, 1 1/2 to 2 hours.

Fry Bread: Mix together flour, milk, baking powder and salt; add shortening. Rub with fingers until coarse crumbs form. Add water and stir with fork until dough clings together. Knead dough on lightly floured board 2 to 3 minutes until smooth. Divide dough into 6 equal portions; keep covered. One portion at at time, shape into a ball, pat onto floured board to 7" round; cover and repeat with remaining dough. In a 9" x 2" skillet, heat 3/4" oil to 375 degrees. Fry bread, turning only once, about 1 1/2 to 2 minutes, until puffy and golden brown. Keep warm in a 200 degree oven, single layer, until all are cooked.

Taco Assembly: Slice a thin section off top and bottom of each tomato. Cut tomatoes crosswise into 1/8" thickness. On each slice, make a cut from edge just to center; set aside. Lay each piece of hot fry bread, cupped side up, on a plate. Spoon chili equally onto fry bread. Top with cheese, lettuce and green onions. Arrange 1 or 2 tomato slices on top each taco. Hold each slice on opposites of center cut, and fold flaps in opposite directions to form a base so the uncut half of the slice sets upright. Set on lettuce. Top with salsa and sour cream.

"These take all day to make but are well worth the effort!"

Beth Kolberg-Bentle   **Rancho High School, North Las Vegas, NV**

Old El Paso Taco Pie

Serves 6

> 5 (fajita size) flour tortillas
> 2 cups jack cheese, shredded
> 1 (4 ounce) can green chiles, chopped
> 1 pound ground beef
> 1 package taco seasoning mix
> 1 cup picante sauce (thick and chunky style)
> 1 egg, beaten
> 1 cup tortilla chips, broken
> 1/2 cup sour cream
> 1 (4 ounce) can olives, sliced
> *Garnish:* sour cream, sliced olives, jalapeño slices

Grease a 9" pie pan. Cut tortillas into fourths. Line bottom and sides of pan with tortilla pieces, overlapping to cover bottom of pan. Sprinkle 1/2 cup cheese over tortillas, top with chiles and set aside. In large skillet, brown beef; drain fat. Add taco seasoning and picante sauce. Cook over low heat 5 to 8 minutes. Remove from heat and add beaten egg. Pour mixture into pan, spreading up to to edge of tortillas. Top with remaining cheese. Sprinkle broken chips over top. Bake at 350 degrees for 20 to 25 minutes. Garnish as desired.

"For a vegetarian dish, use a 16 ounce can of refried beans for the ground beef."

Robin Ali   **Nevada Union High School, Grass Valley, CA**

Olé Brunch Casserole

Serves 6

- 1 pound ground beef
- 1 onion, chopped
- 1/2 teaspoon salt
- 1/4 teaspoon pepper
- 2 (4 ounce) cans green chiles, whole, cut in half crosswise, seeded
- 1 1/2 cups sharp cheddar cheese, shredded
- 1/4 cup flour
- 4 eggs, beaten
- 1 1/2 cups milk
- 1/2 teaspoon hot pepper sauce

Brown meat and onions; drain fat. Add salt and pepper. Place 1/2 of chiles in 10" x 6" x 1 1/2" dish and sprinkle with cheese. Top with beef mixture. Arrange remaining chiles over beef. Combine remaining ingredients and beat until smooth. Pour over chiles. Bake at 350, 40-45 minutes. Cool 5 to 10 minutes. Cut into squares and serve.

"Great Sunday brunch or Cinco de Mayo treat."

Linda Paskins   **Cordova High School, Rancho Cordova, CA**

Olive Mexican Fiesta

Serves 8

- 1 pound ground beef
- 1/2 cup onion, chopped
- 1 (16 ounce) whole tomatoes
- 1 (8 ounce) can tomato sauce
- 1 envelope chili or enchilada sauce
- 1 (15 ounce) can red kidney beans, drained
- 1 can whole kernel corn, drained
- 1 can green chiles, diced
- 1 can ripe olives
- 1 package corn tortilla chips
- 1 cup cheddar cheese, shredded

Brown ground beef and onions; drain fat. Add tomatoes, tomato sauce and chili sauce mix; mix well. Add beans, corn, chiles and olives. In a 2 quart of 9" x 13" baking dish, place a thin layer of crushed tortilla chips. Top with alternating layers of meat mixture and crushed chips, ending with meat. Sprinkle top with cheese and arrange tortilla chips around edges. Bake at 400 degrees for 15 minutes or until cheese is melted.

"Quick and easy—excellent for pot lucks or other large gatherings."

Kay Linberger   **Tokay High School, Lodi, CA**

Picadillo Chile Rellenos

Serves 6 - 8

6 to 8 large Pablano chiles
Picadillo filling:
1 pound lean ground beef
3 tablespoons white onion, minced
salt and pepper, to taste
$1/2$ cup raisins
$1/4$ cup almonds, blanched and minced
Sauce:
1 teaspoon olive oil
2 tablespoons white onion, minced
2 (8 ounce) cans tomato sauce
$1/4$ cup sour cream

Roast chiles on a baking sheet 2" under broiler, turning often, until all sides are blistered. Place chiles in a plastic bag and let stand about 10 minutes, or until cool enough to handle. Peel under cold running water and make a slit to remove seeds. Dry on paper towels and set aside. Prepare filling: cook ground beef and onion in skillet until meat is browned and onion is tender; drain excess fat. Add salt and pepper to taste. Stir in raisins and almonds and cook 2 minutes more. Stuff each chile with hot filling. Place in microwave safe serving dish; set aside. In a saucepan, heat olive oil. Cook onion until transparent. Add tomato sauce and simmer 2 to 3 minutes (a little water may be added if sauce is too thick). Remove from heat and stir in sour cream. Spoon over stuffed chiles.

"This recipe was given to me by my former Spanish teacher, Luz Loza.
The flavors are wonderful!"

Terri Gravison   **Las Plumas High School, Oroville, CA**

Santa Fe Casserole

Serves 5

1 pound lean ground beef
1 can cream-style corn
1 tablespoon chili powder
$1/2$ teaspoon red pepper
1 (10.75 ounce) can cheddar cheese soup
$3/4$ cup green onion, chopped
$3/4$ cup fresh tomatoes, chopped
1 (4 ounce) can green chiles, diced
16 (6 ") corn tortillas
1 cup jack cheese, shredded
$1/2$ cup black olives, sliced

Preheat oven to 350 degrees. Cook ground beef in a large nonstick skillet over medium-high heat until no longer pink; drain excess fat. Stir in creamed corn, chili powder and red pepper. In a large bowl, stir together soup, onion, tomatoes and chiles until blended. Cut tortillas in half. Line bottom of an 11" x 7" with 8 tortilla halves. Cover with half the meat mixture. Repeat layers, ending with soup mixture.

Bake 20 minutes, until tortillas are softened. Top with shredded cheese and olives; bake 10 minutes longer.

"A family favorite–easy and colorful."

Claudia Lening   **Chino High School, Chino, CA**

Scrambled Egg and Hot Dog Burritos

Serves 4

> 8 tablespoons milk
> 8 eggs
> 1/4 teaspoon salt
> 1/4 teaspoon pepper
> 2 tablespoons butter
> 4 hot dogs, sliced or chopped
> 8 flour tortillas

Mix milk with eggs, salt and pepper in a bowl. Melt 1 tablespoon butter in skillet and cook eggs. While eggs cook, melt remaining butter in another skillet and saute hot dogs until browned. Add hot dogs to scrambled eggs and mix together. Warm tortillas in microwave, 4 at a time for 20 seconds. Fill each tortilla with mixture and fold burrito-style. Serve immediately or refrigerate and heat in microwave later (1 1/2 to 2 minutes on HIGH).

"You can spice up the filling with any of your favorite relishes or herbs."

Nan Paul   **Grant Middle School, Escondido, CA**

Shredded Beef

Makes 3 cups

> 2 pounds boneless beef chuck
> 1/4 cup water
> 3 tablespoons red wine vinegar
> 1 1/2 cups beef broth
> 2 tablespoons chili powder
> 1 teaspoon ground cumin

Trim and discard most of the fat from beef chuck. Place meat in a 5 to 6 quart pan with water. Cover and cook 30 minutes. Uncover and cook until liquid almost boils away and meat is well browned; turn as needed. Add vinegar, beef broth, chili powder and ground cumin. Bring to a boil, cover and simmer over medium heat until meat is very tender and easily pulled apart, about 2 hours. Let meat cool, then tear into shreds. Mix with pan juices.

"This can be used as filling for enchiladas, tacos or quesadillas. Delicious!"

Donna Small   **Santana High School, Santee, CA**

Shredded Beef In Crock Pot

Makes 3 pounds

1 (3 pound) tri-tip roast
1 (14 ounce) can chicken or beef broth
1 tablespoon chili powder
1 tablespoon cumin
salt and pepper, to taste

Place all ingredients together in a crock pot. Cook 6 to 8 hours. Shred beef with a fork and use in all your Mexican dishes that call for shredded beef.

"I make this in large quantities and freeze small portions in plastic containers to use as needed for quick and easy Mexican dishes."

Angela Croce　　　　　　　　　**Mira Mesa High School, San Diego, CA**

Shredded Beef With Salsa

Serves 4

1 jar picante sauce
1 beef roast

Put picante sauce and roast in crock pot; cook on low all day. Shred roast and use in tacos, enchiladas, salads or whatever you wish.

"This is a very easy way to have delicious shredded beef."

Marla Hansen　　　　　　　　　**West High School, Tracy, CA**

Sopes

Makes 6

1/2 pound ground beef
1/4 cup frozen mixed vegetables
salt, pepper and garlic powder, to taste
6 sopes
vegetable oil, for frying
1 small can refried beans
1/2 head cabbage, shredded
1 cup cotija cheese, crumbled
1/2 small tomato, sliced
1/2 cup sour cream
1/2 cup salsa

Saute ground beef 5 minutes; drain fat. Add vegetables and spices; cook until vegetables are tender. Fry sopes in 1" oil until golden. Layer sopes with beans, beef, cabbage, cheese, tomato, sour cream and salsa.

"Sopes can be found in the refrigerator section of a Mexican food market. They are worth the effort and easy to make."

Diane Lizardi　　　　　　　　　**Downey High School, Downey, CA**

Fiesta Rice Quesadillas
A layered favorite!
Page 14

Mexi-Lamb Tortilla Lasagna
Lasagna with a Mexican twist!
Page 88

Sundance Pizza Stack
Great for a party!
Page 19

Baja Pizza Pouch
Try this for a party
appetizer or entreé!
Page 75

South of the Border Beef & Corn Casserole

Serves 6

1/2 cup onion, chopped
1/2 cup green pepper, chopped
1 tablespoon butter
1 pound ground beef
2 tablespoons parsley, chopped
1/2 cup raisins
1/3 cup green olives, sliced
salt and pepper, to taste
1 egg, hard boiled, chopped
1 egg, separated
1 (12 ounce) can cream-style corn

Saute onion and green pepper in butter until lightly browned. Add ground beef and cook, stirring constantly until beef is crumbly; drain fat. Add parsley, raisins, olives, salt and pepper; cook until heated through. Pour into baking dish and sprinkle with chopped hard-boiled egg. Combine egg yolk with corn in bowl; mix well. Beat egg white in another bowl until stiff peaks form. Fold into corn mixture. Spoon over casserole and bake at 375 degrees for 30 minutes, until golden brown.

"Easy, delicious main dish! Easy to transport to pot lucks!"

Leilani Neiner   **Fontana High School, Fontana, CA**

Spanish Steak Casserole

Serves 6

2 1/2 pounds round steak, 1" thick
1 1/4 pounds small round potatoes, quartered
1 large onion, chopped
1 cup small pimento-stuffed olives
1 cup chili sauce or salsa
2 beef bouillon cubes
1/4 teaspoon hot sauce
1/2 cup water

Cut meat into 6 serving pieces. Place meat in bottom of a 3 quart casserole, top with potatoes, onion and olives. In a medium saucepan, heat chili sauce, bouillon, hot sauce and water to boiling; pour mixture over casserole. Cover and bake 2 hours or until meat is fork tender.

"Serve this with salad and sourdough bread–great weekend meal after the big Saturday projects!"

Margaret McLeod   **Nogales High School, La Puente, CA**

Speedy Chili

Serves 4

1 pound hamburger
1/2 onion, diced
2 cans chili beans
1 (30 ounce) can tomato sauce
1 tablespoon worcestershire sauce
1 tablespoon chili powder
1/2 teaspoon cumin
1/2 teaspoon oregano
1/2 teaspoon salt

Brown hamburger with onion; drain fat. Drain liquid from beans and add to beef. Stir in remaining ingredients and simmer, over low heat for 10 minutes.

"This can be done in one class period. My high school students love this. It is one of their favorite labs."

Kris Haas   **West Jordan High School, West Jordan, UT**

Spicy Green Enchiladas

Serves 8

3/4 pound hamburger
1/2 medium onion, chopped
1 teaspoon garlic
1 (16 ounce) carton sour cream
1 can Campbell's Cream of Chicken soup
2 (4 ounce) cans green chiles, diced
2 cups cheddar cheese, shredded
nonstick cooking spray
8 (small or medium) flour tortillas
16 black olives, sliced

Brown hamburger; drain excess fat. Add onion and garlic and cook until soft; set aside. In a saucepan, mix together sour cream, soup, green chiles and 1 cup cheese. Remove 1 cup mixture and set aside. Mix remaining mixture with meat. Spray an 11 3/4" x 7 1/2" x 1 3/4" glass baking dish with nonstick cooking spray. Fill each tortilla with 1/4 to 1/2 cup filling and roll. Place in pan, seam side down. Spread reserved 1 cup sour cream mixture over tortillas, covering all. Sprinkle with 1 cup remaining cheese and top with olives. Bake at 350 degrees for 35 minutes.

"To lower fat, substitute ground turkey for hamburger, use nonfat cheese and nonfat sour cream."

Teresa Stahl   **Needles High School, Needles, CA**

Strip Steak With Chili Diablo Sauce

Serves 2

Sauce:
nonstick cooking spray
2 tablespoons green onion, chopped
2 tablespoons green bell pepper, chopped
1/2 cup chili or picante sauce
2 tablespoons red wine vinegar
1/2 teaspoon instant beef bouillon
1/2 teaspoon chili powder
Steaks:
2 (4 to 6 ounce) boneless New York strip beef steaks
1/4 teaspoon salt
1/4 teaspoon black pepper blend

Spray a large nonstick skillet with nonstick cooking spray. Cook onion and bell pepper; stirring over medium heat for 3 to 4 minutes or until crisp tender. Reduce heat to low; stir in remaining sauce ingredients. Cook 3 to 5 minutes or until slightly thickened, stirring occasionally. Sprinkle steaks with salt and pepper blend. Place on broiler pan and broil 4 to 6" from heat or grill on barbecue for 5 to 8 minutes, until desired doneness, turning as needed. Serve sauce with steaks.

"Serve with corn on the cob and a Guacamole Tomato Salad."

Dotti Jones   **Etiwanda High School, Etiwanda, CA**

Stuffed Sour Cream Tacos

Serves 6

2 pounds ground beef
1 medium onion, chopped
2 packages enchilada sauce mix, prepared according to package directions
1 pint sour cream
1/8 teaspoon garlic powder
1/8 teaspoon onion powder
12 corn tortillas
2 (7 ounce) cans ortega green chiles, whole
2 cups Monterey Jack cheese, shredded

Brown ground beef and onions; drain excess fat. In large pan, prepare enchilada sauce as directed on package; heat. Add cooked beef mixture, sour cream, garlic powder and onion powder to enchilada sauce; heat through. Fry tortillas in oil until soft. Spread layer of meat sauce on bottom of a 13" x 9" baking dish. Lay a tortilla in dish and fill with a whole Ortega chile; top with cheese and roll up, placing seam side down. Continue until all tortillas are filled. Pour meat sauce over top and bake at 375 degrees for 20 minutes.

Amy Bame   **Tracy High School, Tracy, CA**

Taco "Goop"

Serves 4 - 6

1 clove garlic, finely chopped
1/2 cup onion, chopped
1/4 cup green pepper, chopped
1 tablespoon oil
1 to 1 1/2 pounds ground beef
2 cans kidney beans, drained
1 (large) can tomato sauce
1/2 teaspoon lemon juice or vinegar
1 teaspoon sugar
1 teaspoon Pico-Pico sauce, or to taste
2 tablespoons worcestershire sauce
salt and pepper, to taste
corn tortillas
oil, for frying
Garnish: grated Parmesan cheese, shredded lettuce

Simmer garlic, onion and green pepper in oil until tender. Add ground beef and cook, stirring to break up, until done; drain fat. Mash kidney beans and add to beef. Stir in tomato sauce, lemon juice or vinegar, sugar, Pico-Pico sauce, worcestershire and salt and pepper. Simmer, covered, most of the day, stirring occasionally, until mixture becomes consistency of mush. (You may hurry along this process by removing the pan lid.) Fry tortillas in oil until crisp; drain on paper towels. Fill tortillas with several spoonfuls of mixture, add Parmesan cheese and finely shredded lettuce.

"Eat with a tea towel bib! My mother, Esther Chandler, made up this recipe. It was a family favorite and won her the honor of Lakeside's Homemaker of the Week."

Nancy Earnest   **Victor Valley High School, Victorville, CA**

Texas Chili

Serves 4

1 (1 1/4 pound) chuck eye steak, boneless
2 medium onions, chopped
2 cloves garlic, minced
2 (15 ounce) cans red kidney beans, drained
2 (15 ounce) cans tomato sauce
6 tablespoons chili powder (or more to taste)
Garnish: chopped green onion, shredded cheese

Remove fat from steak. In large Dutch oven, heat fat. Meanwhile, cut meat into small pieces. Brown meat in hot fat. Remove meat and set aside. Cook onion and garlic in small amount of fat until soft. Pour off any remaining fat. Return meat to Dutch oven. Add remaining ingredients and simmer for 15 minutes. Taste for seasonings and garnish as desired.

Cynthia Figueiredo   **A.B. Miller High School, Fontana, CA**

Tijuana Torte

Serves 6 - 8

    1 pound ground beef
    1 medium onion, chopped
    1 (16 ounce) can stewed tomatoes
    1 (8 ounce) can tomato sauce
    1 (4 ounce) can green chiles, diced
    1 package Lawry's Taco Seasoning Mix
    12 corn tortillas
    1 pound cheddar cheese, shredded

Brown ground beef with onion in skillet; drain fat. Add stewed tomatoes, tomato sauce, chiles and taco seasoning; simmer 10 to 15 minutes. Place 1/4 cup of meat mixture in bottom of a 9" x 13" baking dish. Place two tortillas side by side on meat mixture. Top each tortilla with some meat mixture and shredded cheese. Repeat until each stack contains 6 tortillas layered with meat and cheese. Bake at 350 degrees for 20 to 25 minutes. Cut each stack into quarters to serve.

"I got this recipe on a tour of Lawry's Kitchen more than twenty years ago and my students enjoy this one!"

Amber Bradley   **Granite Hills High School, El Cajon, CA**

Tostada Lada

Serves 5 - 6

    1 pound ground beef
    1 small onion, chopped
    1 (16 ounce) can refried beans
    16 ounces cheddar cheese, shredded
    1 (32 ounce) can enchilada sauce
    5 to 6 corn tortillas
    1/2 head lettuce, chopped
    1 to 2 tomatoes, chopped
    1 (small) can olives, chopped
    2 to 3 green olives, chopped

Cook ground beef and onion; drain fat. Return to pan; add refried beans, 1/2 of the cheese and half of the enchilada sauce. Heat remaining enchilada sauce in medium saucepan. Dip each corn tortilla in heated sauce and place on a plate. Top with about 1/2 cup meat mixture. Sprinkle with shredded cheese, lettuce, tomatoes onions and olives.

"A quick to fix recipe that really fills you up!"

Paula Schaefer   **Garside Middle School, Las Vegas, NV**

Tri-Tip Burritos

Serves 4

1 (2 1/2 to 3 pound) tri tip roast
1 jar salsa
1 medium onion, chopped
1 medium bell pepper, chopped
1/2 cup liquid (water, beef broth, etc.)

Trim excess fat from roast. Place in crockpot. Add remaining ingredients and cook all day on medium setting. Remove meat from crockpot and shred with a fork; discard liquid. Serve in warm tortillas.

"Great for pot lucks!"

Karin Hitchen **Arroyo Grande High School, Arroyo Grande, CA**

Upside Down Mexican Sloppy Joes

Serves 5 - 6

Corn Dough:
1 cup Bisquick baking mix
1/2 cup yellow cornmeal
1/2 cup milk
1 (7 ounce) can whole kernel corn, drained
Filling:
1 pound ground beef
1/2 cup green onions, sliced, with tops
1/2 cup green pepper, chopped
1/2 cup water
3 tablespoons green chiles, diced
1 (8 ounce) jar taco sauce
1 (8 ounce) can tomato sauce
1 (8 ounce) jar mild picante sauce

Prepare corn dough: mix Bisquick and cornmeal and milk together until dough forms. Stir in drained corn; set aside. Meanwhile, prepare filling by browning ground beef with onion in 10" skillet; drain fat. Stir in remaining ingredients. Cover and heat to boiling over medium-low heat. Drop corn dough by heaping spoonfuls onto boiling beef mixture. Cook, uncovered,10 minutes. Cover and cook 10 minutes longer. Serve hot.

"This recipe comes from Bisquick Cookbook. *Simple and delicious!"*

Darlene V. Brown **Golden Valley Middle School, San Bernardino, CA**

Arroz Con Pollo Burritos

Serves 6 - 8

2 1/2 cups chicken, cooked, shredded
1 (1.0 ounce) Lawry's Taco Spices & Seasonings
3 1/4 cups water
2 tablespoons vegetable oil
1 cup long grain rice
1 (8 ounce) can tomato sauce
1 teaspoon Lawry's Lemon Pepper Seasoning
1 large tomato, chopped
1/4 cup green onion, chopped
6 (8") flour tortillas, warmed
cheddar cheese, shredded
Garnish: salsa, guacamole

Photo Opposite
Page 64

In large deep skillet, combine chicken, Taco Spices & Seasonings and 3/4 cup water. Bring to a boil; reduce heat and simmer, uncovered, 10 minutes. Remove and set aside. In same skillet, heat oil. Add rice; saute until golden. Add remaining 2-1/2 cups water, tomato sauce and Lemon Pepper Seasoning. Bring to a boil; reduce heat, cover and simmer 20 minutes. Stir in chicken, tomato and green onion; blend well. Heat 5 minutes. Place a heaping 1/2 cup filling on each tortilla. Fold in sides and roll to enclose filling. Place filled burritos on baking sheet; seam side down. Sprinkle with cheese. Heat in 350 degree oven for 5 minutes to melt cheese. Garnish as desired. Note: 1 pound ground beef, browned and drained can be substituted for cooked chicken.

Lawry's Foods, Inc.   **www.lawrys.com**

Bronco Fajitas

Serves 4

1 pound chicken breast halves, skinless, cut into strips
1 tablespoon corn oil
2 tablespoons lemon juice
1 teaspoon garlic powder
1 teaspoon seasoned salt
$1/2$ teaspoon ground oregano
$1/2$ teaspoon pepper
1/8 teaspoon liquid smoke flavoring
3 tablespons olive oil
1 cup green bell pepper, cut into strips
1 cup onion wedges, thinly sliced
1 cup tomato wedges, thinly sliced
$1/2$ cup salsa
8 corn or flour tortillas, heated

In medium bowl, combine chicken strips with corn oil, lemon juice, garlic powder, seasoned salt, oregano, pepper and liquid smoke; cover and refrigerate 8 to 10 hours. In a 10" skillet, heat olive oil over high heat until very hot. Saute half of the chicken until no longer pink, about 30 seconds. Add half of green pepper and onion and continue cooking 1 to 2 minutes; remove from skillet. Repeat with remaining meat, pepper and onion, adding additional oil if needed. Return all of meat, pepper and onion to skillet. Add tomato and salsa; simmer, tossing meat and vegetables 1 minute longer. Serve immediately in heated tortillas.

"Serve these with refried beans and rice."

Denise Stallman   **Rancho Bernardo High School, San Diego, CA**

Chicken Asparagus Casserole

Serves 8

nonstick cooking spray
1 can cream of asparagus soup
$1/2$ soup can milk
$1/2$ pint sour cream
12 corn tortillas
8 chicken breast halves, cooked, shredded into bite-sized pieces
1 can green chiles, diced
1 pound cheddar cheese, shredded
1 can ripe olives, sliced

Spray a 16" x 11" pan with nonstick cooking spray. In a bowl, combine soup, milk and sour cream. Cover bottom of pan with a layer of soup mixture, then 2 layers of tortillas, a layer of chicken, a layer of green chiles, then a layer of cheese; repeat. Sprinkle with sliced olives. Bake at 350 degrees for 1 hour.

"I lower fat by using nonfat milk, sour cream and jack cheese.
Flour tortillas may also be substituted for corn."

Jill Sweet-Gregory   **Santa Paula High School, Santa Paula, CA**

Chicken Enchiladas In Green Sauce

Serves 4

    2 tablespoons oil
    1/2 cup onion, chopped
    1 (4ounce) can green chiles, diced
    2 cups chicken or turkey, cooked, cubed
    1 (24 ounce) can green chile enchilada sauce
    3 cups cheddar cheese, grated
    8 corn tortillas

Heat oil in a skillet. Add onions and green chiles and saute for 5 minutes. Remove from heat; add chicken, 1 1/4 cups enchilada sauce and 1 cup cheese. Mix well. Warm tortillas in microwave and divide filling into center of each tortilla, about 1/2 cup each. Roll up and place, seam side down, in 12" x 8" baking dish. Pour remaining enchilada sauce over all the enchiladas. Cover with foil and bake at 350 degrees for 20 minutes. Remove foil, garnish with remaining cheese and heat 10 minutes more.

"Great way to use up leftover turkey or chicken."

Sue Waterbury   **San Luis Obispo High School, San Luis Obispo, CA**

Chicken Enchiladas in Salsa Verde

Serves 8

    Salsa Verde:
    1 (24 ounce) can tomatillos
    1 bunch cilantro, chopped
    3 whole chile peppers (from can of jalapeños en escabeche), seeded, chopped
    1 clove garlic, finely chopped
    1/2 onion, chopped
    3 tablespoons parsley, coarsely chopped
    1/2 teaspoon salt
    1 pinch sugar
    2 tablespoons shortening
    Enchiladas:
    12 corn tortillas
    4 whole chicken breast halves, skinned, cooked, shredded
    1 1/2 pounds Monterey Jack cheese, shredded
    1 (14 ounce) can olives, coarsely chopped
    1/2 cup light cream
    1 bunch scallions, chopped (whites only)
    1 cup sour cream

Drain the tomatillos (saving the liquid for use if the salsa is too thick) and place them in a large mixing bowl with cilantro, chiles, garlic, onion, parsley, salt and sugar. Pour 1/2 of mixture into the container of an electric blender; blend until smooth. Repeat with remaining mixture. In a heavy 10" skillet, melt the shortening over medium heat; add salsa. Bring sauce to a boil, reduce heat and simmer for 5 minutes. Dip a tortilla into warm salsa verde for a few seconds until limp. Laying the tortilla on a flat surface, assemble enchilada by putting 2 tablespoons shredded chicken, 2 tablespoons shredded cheese and 1 tablespoon chopped olives in center of tortilla. Roll up and place seam side down in a shallow 9" x 13" casserole dish. Repeat with remaining tortillas. Pour the cream around and under the enchiladas, lifting the edges with a spatula to permit the cream to run under. Cover enchiladas with remaining salsa and shredded cheese. Top with chopped scallions. Bake, uncovered, in preheated 350 degree oven for 20 minutes. Top with a spoonful of sour cream.

Note: The enchiladas should not be assembled more than 1 hour ahead of time, as they absorb liquid and become limp. You can freeze the enchiladas once you have them assembled, but do not add the cream or salsa to topping before freezing.

"I often have the salsa in the freezer for a quick meal or use Las Palmas brand green chile enchilada sauce instead."

Chris Henry   **Rancho Starbuck Intermediate School, Whittier, CA**

Chicken Fajitas with Cilantro Cream

Serves 6

Cilantro Cream:
2 - 3 tablespoons fresh cilantro, chopped
$1/2$ cup sour cream
1 tablespoon red onion, finely chopped
1 tablespoon fresh jalapeño pepper, seeded, finely chopped
1 tablespoon fresh lime juice
$1/4$ teaspoon salt
Fajitas:
3 teaspoons olive oil
4 boneless, skinless chicken breast halves, cut into thin strips
1 (each) red, yellow and green peppers, thinly sliced
1 medium onion, thinly sliced
$1/2$ teaspoon salt
$1/4$ teaspoon pepper
2 tablespoons chili powder
$1/2$ teaspoon cumin
$1/2$ cup chicken broth
12 flour tortillas

Prepare cilantro cream by whisking ingredients together; refrigerate. Heat oil in large skillet over medium-high heat. Add chicken; saute until lightly browned, about 7 to 8 minutes. Remove chicken from skillet and set aside. Add peppers and onions, sauteeing for 8 minutes, or until softened. Add cooked chicken, salt, pepper, chili powder, cumin and chicken broth; simmer for 8 minutes or until liquid is gone. Wrap flour tortillas in aluminum foil. Heat in 400 degree oven for 10 minutes. Spoon $3/4$ cup chicken mixture into center of warmed flour tortilla. Roll up and place on a platter. Repeat with remaining tortillas and filling. Top each with cilantro cream and serve.

Penny Childers   **Ramona High School, Ramona, CA**

Chicken Spinach Enchiladas

Makes 12

> 1/2 package frozen spinach, chopped, cooked, well drained
> 1 can cream of chicken soup
> 1 can "Aunt Penneys" white sauce
> 1 (4 ounce) can green chiles, diced
> 12 (12" burrito size) flour tortillas
> 4 to 6 chicken breast halves, cooked, diced
> 1 pound jack cheese, shredded
> 5 to 6 green onions, chopped
> 1 pound Tillamook cheese, shredded

In blender, mix spinach, soup, white sauce and green chiles to make a sauce. Coat a tortilla with sauce on both sides. Place diced chicken, jack cheese, green onion and 1 tablespoon sauce inside tortilla and roll up, placing seam side down in 13" x 9" greased pan. Continue until all tortillas are used. Pour remaining sauce over top, sprinkle with Tillamook cheese and bake, covered, at 350 degrees for 30 minutes .

"Thanks to Rita Berdelis for sharing this recipe with the Warren Staff."
Rhonda Nelson   **Rancho Santa Margarita Intermediate School, RSM, CA**

Chicken Taco Pie

Serves 6

> 1 (1 1/2 pound) chicken, cooked
> 1 cup reserved chicken broth
> 1 large can enchilada sauce
> 1 can mushroom soup
> 1 large onion, chopped
> 1/2 teaspoon garlic, minced
> dash pepper
> 1 (11 ounce) package Fritos
> 1 cup cheddar cheese, shredded

Remove meat from bones of chicken; discard bones and shred meat into bite-sized pieces. Combine chicken with enchilada sauce, soup, onion, garlic and pepper. Line a 9" x 13" x 2" dish with 1/2 of the Fritos. Pour chicken mixture over Fritos and sprinkle with shredded cheese. Top with remaining Fritos. Pour reserved 1 cup chicken broth over top and bake at 350 degrees for 30 minutes.

"Always a hit and so quick and easy to make for the person in a hurry."
Roberta Hawkes   **A.B. Miller High School, Fontana, CA**

Chicken Tacos

Makes 12

  1 clove garlic
  1/2 teaspoon salt
  1 tablespoon vegetable oil
  1 onion, chopped
  1 to 2 tomatoes, chopped
  pinch pepper
  1/8 teaspoon ground cumin
  3 1/2 to 4 cups chicken, cooked and shredded
  12 to 15 taco shells
  Garnish: 1/2 head shredded lettuce, 1 1/4 cups shredded cheese, sour cream

Mash garlic with salt to make a paste. Heat oil in a large skillet; add onion and garlic paste. Cook until onion is tender. Add tomatoes, pepper and cumin. Stir in chicken. Cook and stir until mixture is fairly dry. Fill taco shells with chicken mixture. Serve with garnishes.

Diana Lee   **David A. Brown Middle School, Wildomar, CA**

Chicken Tostadas

Serves 8

  1 pound boneless chicken breast halves, cut into 1/2" cubes
  1 tablespoon oil
  1 small onion, finely chopped
  1 clove garlic, minced
  1 jalapeño chile, minced (optional)
  1 (10 ounce) can enchilada sauce
  1 (1 pound) can refried beans
  2 to 4 green chiles, sliced
  1 cup jack cheese, shredded
  3 cups lettuce, shredded
  2 green onions, sliced
  1 cup cheddar cheese, shredded
  1/2 cup salsa
  2 tablespoons Italian salad dressing
  4 to 8 corn tortillas
  oil for frying

Heat 1 tablespoon oil in skillet and saute chicken until no longer pink. Add onion, garlic and jalapeño. Stir in enchilada sauce and bring to a boil. Lower temperature and simmer until ready to serve. In a greased casserole (1 1/2 quart) layer on half of the beans, onions and jack cheese; repeat. Cover and bake at 350 degrees for 30 minutes or microwave on HIGH about 7 minutes. In a bowl, mix lettuce, green onions, cheddar cheese and salsa. Toss with salad dressing just before serving. Heat oil for frying. Fry tortillas until crisp, drain on paper towels.To serve: place a tortilla on plate, top with beans, then chicken, then salad.

"All of my students and my friends love this recipe! It's so delicious!"

Gail Hurt   **Estancia High School, Costa Mesa, CA**

Chile Chicken

Serves 4

> 3 cans cream of chicken soup
> 2 cups cooked chicken, diced
> 3 cups cheddar or longhorn cheese, shredded
> 1 (7 ounce) can green chiles, diced
> 1 cup evaporated milk
> $^1/_2$ to 1 package tortilla or corn chips

Mix all ingredients together in a greased 2 quart casserole dish. The chips thicken so you can use less milk and less chips. Bake at 350 degrees for 30 to 45 minutes, until set.

> *"This is a super quick and easy dish to serve. Great for pot lucks.*
> *Try all lowfat products to reduce the fat."*

Jan Katcher   **Rhodes Junior High School, Mesa, AZ**

Chili Chicken Casserole

Serves 8 - 10

> 1 cup sour cream
> $^1/_2$ cup ricotta cheese
> 1 (3 ounce) package cream cheese
> 3 cups chicken, cooked, chopped
> 3 cups rice, cooked
> 1 $^1/_2$ cups Monterey Jack cheese, shredded
> 1 (10.75 ounce) can cream of chicken soup
> 1 (4 ounce) can green chiles, diced
> 1 (15 ounce) can tomatoes, chopped
> 1 (15 ounce) can black beans, rinsed, drained
> $^1/_2$ teaspoon garlic salt
> 1 cup tortilla chips, coarsely crushed

Blend together sour cream, ricotta cheese and cream cheese until smooth. Add all remaining ingredients except tortilla chips. Pour into an ungreased shallow 9" x 13" casserole baking dish. Sprinkle with tortilla chips. Bake at 350 degrees for 30 minutes.

> *"My personal adaptation of a recipe put out by the Wisconsin Milk Board."*

Elaine Thomas   **Hollencrest Middle School, West Covina, CA**

Ensenada Fish Tacos

Makes 6

Photo on
Front Cover

10 ounces halibut or orange roughly, cut into 1" cubes
1 tablespoon vegetable oil
1 tablespoon lime juice
1 (1.27 ounce) Lawry's Spices & Seasonings for Fajitas
6 (8") corn or flour tortillas
2 1/2 cups lettuce, shredded
1/2 cup tomatoes, diced
3/4 cup Monterey Jack or cheddar cheese, shredded
2 tablespoons green onion, thinly sliced
Garnish: sour cream, guacamole, salsa, fresh cilantro

Place fish in a shallow glass baking dish. Pour oil and lime juice over fish. Sprinkle with Lawry's Spices & Seasonings for Fajitas; toss lightly to coat. Cover with plastic wrap and refrigerate 2 hours to marinate, occasionally spooning marinade over fish. Bake fish in 450 degree oven 10 minutes, or until fish flakes easily with fork; drain. To serve, evenly divide fish and place in center of each tortilla. Top with lettuce, tomatoes, cheese and green onion. Garnish as desired.

Lawry's Foods   **Los Angeles, CA**

Favorite Chimichangas

Serves 8

1 tomato, diced
1 onion, diced
3 cloves garlic, minced
2 teaspoon cumin
1 tablespoon oil
1 pound ground turkey or beef
1 (4 ounce) can green chiles, diced
1 1/2 teaspoons salt
1 cup Monterey Jack cheese, shredded
10 to 12 flour tortillas
oil, for frying
Garnish: sour cream, salsa, guacamole, shredded lettuce, chopped tomatoes

Mix tomato, onion, garlic and cumin together. Saute this mixture in 1 tablespoon oil for 3 minutes. Add the ground meat, chiles and salt. Reduce heat and simmer 7 to 8 minutes. To assemble, place 2 tablespoons of mixture and 1 teaspoon cheese in center of each tortilla. Fold up ends of tortilla. Heat electric fry pan to 350 degrees with 1 1/2" oil. Place chimichangas, seam side down in hot oil. Fry until light brown; drain on paper towels. Serve hot with garnishes.

"The students at our school enjoy this recipe!"

Bonnie Landin   **Garden Grove High School, Garden Grove, CA**

Fish Tacos

Serves 4 - 6

1/4 cup cooking oil
1 pound red snapper, cut into bite-sized pieces
1/2 medium onion, chopped
1 medium zucchini sliced and halved
1 medium tomato, chopped
2 cups Monterey Jack cheese, shredded
6 corn or flour tortillas
salsa

Heat oil in large skillet. Stir fry fish with onion, zucchini and tomato until tender. Place a large spoonful of filling on a warmed tortilla. Sprinkle about 1/4 cup shredded cheese over filling. Top with salsa and enjoy!

"I developed this recipe from the fish tacos at a local Mexican restaurant."

Kristine Hubbard   **San Luis Obispo High School, San Luis Obispo, CA**

Fish Vera Cruz

Serves 4

1 1/4 pounds fish fillets, about 1/2" thick
1 tablespoon lime juice
1 medium onion, sliced
1 medium green bell pepper, cut into bite-sized pieces
1 clove garlic, minced
1 tablespoon vegetable oil
2 medium tomatoes, cut into chunks
1/2 cup chili sauce
1/4 cup pimento stuffed olives, sliced
dash ground red pepper

Sprinkle fish with lime juice; set aside. In large skillet, cook and stir onion, green pepper and garlic in oil until tender crisp. Add tomatoes and remaining ingredients. Simmer, uncovered, 3 to 5 minutes or until most of liquid evaporates. Place fish in skillet, spooning sauce over. Cover; simmer 6 to 8 minutes, or until fish turns opaque and begins to flake when tested with fork. Remove fish; simmer sauce to thicken if necessary. Serve sauce over fish.

"Spanish rice goes well with this entree'."

Kathie Baczynski   **Mt. Carmel High School, Poway, CA**

Gazpacho Fillets

Serves 4

1 pound orange roughy fish fillets, thawed, if frozen
1 cup water
1 large tomato
$1/4$ cup cucumber, chopped
$1/4$ cup green pepper, chopped
$1/4$ cup celery, chopped
2 tablespoons onion, chopped
1 tablespoon lemon juice
1 teaspoon sugar
$1/2$ teaspoon instant chicken bouillon granules
dash pepper
dash hot pepper sauce
2 tablespoons tomato sauce or tomato paste

In 2 cup measure, heat water, uncovered on 100% power for 3 minutes, or until boiling. Spear tomato with a fork and carefully dip into hot water for 12 seconds. Hold tomato under cold water until cool enough to handle; remove peel and chop. In microwave dish with lid, stir together tomato with cucumber, green pepper, celery, onion, lemon juice, sugar, bouillon granules, pepper and hot sauce. Arrange thawed fish fillets on top of vegetables with thicker portions toward edges of the dish. Turn under any thin portions of fillets to obtain thickness of about $1/2$". Sprinkle fillets with salt and pepper. Cover with lid or vented clear plastic wrap. Cook on HIGH for 6 to 9 minutes, turning $1/2$ turn after 4 minutes, until fish flakes easily with a fork. Carefully transfer fish to serving dish. Stir tomato paste or tomato sauce into vegetable mixture. Heat, uncovered, on HIGH about 1 minute or until heated through. Pour sauce over fish and serve. Note: You can substitute your favorite retail salsa to make this dish even quicker!

"In my Foods Lab, this is the best way to entice students to try fish. They love it!"
Renee Wilgus **Red Bluff Union High School, Red Bluff, CA**

Grilled Swordfish with Mango Salsa

Serves 6

2 pounds swordfish
Marinade:
juice from 2 limes
2 tablespoons cilantro
salt and pepper, to taste
Salsa:
juice from 1 lime
3 tablespoons cilantro, chopped
2 mangoes, peeled, diced
2 tomatoes, chopped
1 small red onion, diced
1 jalapeño, minced
salt and pepper, to taste
1 teaspoon oil

Marinate fish in marinade 15 to 30 minutes. Grill or barbecue fish until it tests done with a fork. Meanwhile, combine salsa ingredients in a small bowl. Top with salsa.

"This is a refreshing main course for summer."

Cynthia Allen   **Royal High School, Simi Valley, CA**

Gus' Chicken

Serves 4 - 6

1 frying chicken, cut up
3 tablespoons oil
1 can cream of celery soup
1 can cream of asparagus soup
1/2 soup can water
1 (small) can olives, sliced
1 (small) can green chiles, diced
1 bay leaf
1/2 teaspoon oregano
1/2 teaspoon chili powder
pinch dried red chili peppers
1 (small) can mushrooms (optional)
3 cups cooked rice
flour tortillas, warmed, buttered

Brown chicken in oil on all sides over medium-high heat; remove from pan and set aside. In another large skillet, mix remaining ingredients except rice and tortillas over low heat until heated through. Add chicken to skillet; cover and simmer 20 minutes, until juices from chicken run clear. Serve over rice with warm, buttered flour tortillas.

"My husband got this recipe from a college roommate many years ago."

Amy Bean   **Cabrillo High School, Lompoc, CA**

Lowfat Chicken Enchilada Casserole

Serves 8

4 to 6 skinless chicken breast halves, cooked
1 can lowfat cream of chicken soup
1 cup lowfat milk
1 cup green chile salsa
1 large white onion, finely chopped
1 package corn tortillas, cut into 1" strips
2 cups lowfat cheddar cheese, shredded

Shred or dice cooked chicken; set aside. Mix soup, milk, salsa and onion together. Spray a 9" x 13" baking dish with nonstick cooking spray. Line bottom of pan with half the tortilla strips. Next, layer half the chicken and half the sauce, repeating until all ingredients are used.Top with shredded cheese. Cover and refrigerate 24 hours. Bake, uncovered at 300 degrees for 1 1/2 hours.

"Serve with a crisp green salad and lowfat Italian dressing, warm flour tortillas and fresh fruit for dessert. Substitute cooked turkey breast for chicken breast."

Marianne Traw   **Ball Junior High School, Anaheim, CA**

Lowfat Turkey Enchiladas

Serves 6

nonstick cooking spray
1/2 cup onion, chopped
1/2 of (8 ounce) package light cream cheese, softened
3/4 teaspoon ground cumin
4 cups turkey, cooked
1/4 cup pecans, toasted, chopped
12 (6 ") flour tortillas
1 (10.75) ounce can reduced sodium cream of chicken soup
1 (8 ounce) carton light sour cream
1 cup skim milk
1 to 2 tablespoons mild jalapeño pepper strips, finely chopped
1/2 cup reduced fat sharp cheddar cheese, shredded

Cook onion, covered, in small amount of water in small skillet over medium heat until tender; drain. Spray a 13" x 9" x 2" baking dish with nonstick cooking spray. Stir together cream cheese, cumin and 1 tablespoon water. Stir in cooked onion, turkey and pecans. Wrap tortillas in foil and heat in 350 degree oven 10 to 15 minutes or wrap in paper towels and microwave on high for 30 to 60 seconds. Spoon about 1/4 cup filling on each tortilla; roll up and place seam side down in baking dish. Combine soup, sour cream, milk and pepper strips; pour over filled tortillas. Bake, covered, in 350 degree oven about 40 minutes or until heated through. Sprinkle with cheddar cheese and bake, uncovered 4 to 5 minutes more, until cheese melts.

"This is always a potluck favorite as well as one of our most well-liked family meals. 250 calories and 10 grams fat each!"

Julie Hampton   **Gordon Russell Middle School, Gresham, OR**

Marinade for Grilled Fish

Makes 1 cup

1/2 cup olive oil
3 tablespoons lime juice
1/2 cup cilantro, chopped
1 teaspoon garlic, chopped (or more if desired)

Combine ingredients and place in large plastic ziploc bag with 1 pound of firm-fleshed fish such as halibut or salmon. Marinate for at least 1 hour. Grill approximately 15 minutes per each inch of thickness of fish, or until fish flakes, or follow directions with your grill.

"This great recipe is from my daughter, Kay. With many avid fishermen in the family, this recipe is a favorite of ours."

Myrna Swearingen   **Corona High School, Corona, CA**

Mexican Meatloaf

Serves 6

> 2 pounds ground turkey
> 2/3 cup tortilla chips, crushed
> 1/2 cup onion, chopped
> 4 tablespoons green pepper, chopped
> 2 (1.5 ounce) packages taco seasoning mix
> 2 (15 ounce) cans tomato sauce

Combine all ingredients except tomato sauce. Press mixture into a lightly greased 9" x 5" loaf pan. Bake at 350 degrees for 65 to 70 minutes. When set, remove from pan to a platter. In small saucepan, heat tomato sauce. Slice meatloaf and drizzle heated tomato sauce over each serving.

"This is only 290 calories per serving."

Sonja Tyree   **Ayala High School, Chino, CA**

Mexican-Style Chicken Kiev

Serves 8

> 8 chicken breast halves, skinned and boned
> 1 (7 ounce) can green chiles, diced
> 4 ounces Monterey Jack cheese, cut into 8" strips
> 1/2 cup fine dry bread crumbs
> 1/4 cup Parmesan cheese, grated
> 1 tablespoon chili powder
> 1/2 teaspoon salt
> 1/4 teaspoon ground cumin
> 1/4 teaspoon black pepper
> 6 to 8 tablespoons butter, melted
> *Tomato Sauce:*
> 1 (1 pound) can tomato sauce
> 1/2 teaspoon ground cumin
> 1/3 cup green onion
> salt and pepper, to taste
> hot pepper sauce

Pound chicken breasts to about 1/4" thickness. Put about 2 tablespoons chiles and 1 jack cheese strip in center of each chicken breast. Roll up and tuck ends under. Combine bread crumbs, Parmesan cheese, chili powder, salt, cumin and pepper. Dip chicken in melted butter and roll in crumb mixture. Place chicken rolls, seam side down, in oblong baking dish and drizzle with a little melted butter. Cover and chill 4 hours or overnight. Bake, uncovered at 400 degrees for 20 minutes, or until done. Combine tomato sauce ingredients in saucepan and simmer 5 to 10 minutes. Serve with chicken.

Millie Deeton   **Ayala High School, Chino Hills, CA**

Picante Chicken

Serves 4

    4 chicken breasts, boneless, skinless
    1 teaspoon cumin
    1/2 teaspoon garlic powder
    pepper, to taste
    1 tablespoon oil (optional)
    1 (15 ounce) can black beans, drained, rinsed
    1 cup corn, frozen
    1 1/2 cups Pace picante sauce

Season chicken breasts with cumin, garlic powder and pepper. Brown chicken in oil or omit oil and use nonstick cooking pan. Add beans, corn and picante sauce to pan; reduce heat and cover. Cook 15 minutes, or until fork tender.

Julie Blanchard   **Western High School, Anaheim, CA**

Sandy's Chicken Enchilada Casserole

Serves 5

    1/2 cup onion, minced
    1 (4 ounce) can green chiles, diced
    1 can cream of chicken soup
    1/2 soup can water
    nonstick cooking spray
    1 dozen corn tortillas, cut into quarters
    3 chicken breast halves, cooked, shredded
    1 1/2 cups cheddar cheese, shredded

Combine onion, green chiles, soup and water in a bowl. Spray a 13" x 9" baking pan with nonstick cooking spray. Layer tortillas, chicken, soup mixture and cheese in pan until all ingredients are used. Cover with foil. Bake at 350 degrees for 30 minutes. Serve hot.

"A family favorite."

Reiko Ikkanda   **So. Pasadena Middle School, So. Pasadena, CA**

Shredded Chicken & Black Bean Bake

Serves 4

    1 (7 ounce) package instant black bean mix
    2 cups boiling water
    1/3 to 1/2 cup dry sherry (or more water)
    4 large chicken breast halves, skinned, boned
    2 quarts iceberg lettuce, shredded
    1 cup jack cheese, shredded
    1 fresh red or green jalapeño pepper, thinly sliced crosswise into rings
    Garnish: cherry tomatoes, plain nonfat yogurt or reduced fat sour cream

In a shallow 2 1/2 quart baking dish, stir together instant black bean mix, boiling water and dry sherry (use larger amount if you prefer a saucelike consistency.) Lay chicken breasts slightly apart on top of beans. Bake, uncovered, at 400 degrees until chicken is no longer pink in center of thickest part, about 20 minutes. Stir any excess liquid around chicken into beans. Mound shredded lettuce on 4 dinner plates; place equal portions of beans and chicken on top of lettuce. Sprinkle with shredded cheese and jalapeños. Garnish each plate with cherry tomatoes. Serve with yogurt or sour cream.

"Very impressive meal! Enjoy!"

Brenda Burke   **Mt. Whitney High School, Visalia, CA**

Shrimp Enchiladas Con Queso

Serves 4 - 8

2 tablespoons olive oil, divided
1/2 cup red bell pepper, chopped
1/2 cup onion, minced
1 jalapeño pepper, cored, seeded, minced
1 fresh green chili pepper, seeded, diced
1 small habanero pepper, seeded, chopped (optional)
1/2 teaspoon garlic, minced
1/2 teaspoon dried oregano
1/2 teaspoon salt
pinch freshly ground pepper
pinch cayenne pepper
3 tablespoons flour
3 tablespoons water
1 cup milk
1 cup Monterey Jack cheese, shredded, divided
1/4 cup sour cream
1 pound medium shrimp, peeled and deveined
3/4 cup green onions, chopped, divided
2 medium tomatoes, peeled, seeded, and chopped, divided
8 (8") flour tortillas
Garnishes: guacamole, salsa

Preheat oven to 350 degrees. Grease large baking dish. In large heavy saucepan, heat 1 tablespoon olive oil over medium heat. Add bell pepper, onion, chiles, garlic and oregano; cook until tender, about 5 minutes, stirring occasionally. Stir in salt, pepper and cayenne. Remove from heat. In a small bowl, combine flour and water. Whisk to blend and add to bell pepper mixture. Slowly add milk and stir until well blended. Return pan to medium heat and simmer until slightly thickened, about 3 minutes, stirring constantly. Add 1/2 cup shredded cheese and stir until melted. Remove from heat and stir in sour cream. In large skillet, heat remaining 1 tablespoon oil over high heat. Add shrimp and 1/2 cup of the green onions, Stir until shrimp just turns pink, about 2 minutes. Stir in half of the bell pepper mixture and half of the tomatoes. Remove from heat. Spoon approximately 1/2 cup of shrimp mixture onto 1 tortilla and roll tightly. Place seam side down, in baking dish and repeat with remaining tortillas. (May prepare up to this point 2 hours in advance; cover and chill.) Top enchiladas with remaining half of bell pepper mixture. Cover with foil and bake 30 to 40 minutes, until heated thoroughly. Top with remaining 1/2 cup shredded cheese, 1/4 cup onions and remaining half of tomatoes. Garnish as desired and serve immediately.

"Fabulous! It tastes like something you'd get at an upscale restaurant."
Patti Bartholomew   **Casa Roble High School, Orangevale, CA**

Skillet Enchiladas

Serves 4

    1 pound ground turkey breast
    1/2 cup onion, chopped
    2 tablespoons green chiles, diced
    1 (10.75 ounce) can cream of chicken soup
    1 (10 ounce) can enchilada sauce
    1/3 cup milk
    1/4 cup cooking oil
    8 corn or flour tortillas
    2 1/2 cups American cheese, shredded
    1/2 cup ripe olives, sliced

Brown ground turkey and chopped onion in large skillet. Stir in chiles, soup, enchilada sauce and milk; bring to a boil. Reduce heat. Cover and simmer 20 minutes. Heat cooking oil in a small skillet and fry corn tortillas until they are limp. (If using flour tortillas, heat in microwave oven 2 at a time for 20 to 30 seconds). Drain excess oil from corn tortillas. Place 1/4 cup shredded cheese on each tortilla. (Reserve 1/2 cup cheese for garnish.) Sprinkle with one tablespoon olives in each tortilla. Roll up and place in meat mixture in large skillet. Cover skillet and cook for 5 minutes. Uncover and sprinkle with reserved cheese. Serve hot.

Kathie Hogen   **Hendrix Junior High School, Chandler, AZ**

Slow Cooked Taos Taco Stew

Serves 6

    1 pound boneless, skinless chicken breast, cubed
    1 onion, chopped
    1 clove garlic, pressed
    1 tablespoon parsley, chopped
    1 envelope taco seasoning
    1 (16 ounce) can solid pack tomatoes, with liquid, chopped
    1/2 cup beef or chicken broth
    1 (16 ounce) can pinto beans, drained
    1 (16 ounce) can corn, drained
    1 (7 ounce) can green chiles, diced

Place all ingredients in a crock pot. Cook 8 to 10 hours. Serve with tortillas or tortilla chips.

"Teach all day, then come home to a hearty, delicious dinner!"
Nanci Burkhart   **Hueneme High School, Oxnard, CA**

Sour Cream Chicken Tortilla Casserole

Serves 10

    1/2 cup onion, chopped
    2 tablespoons canola oil
    1 (28 ounce) can tomatoes
    1 package Spanish rice seasoning mix
    2 tablespoons salsa jalapeña
    12 corn tortillas
    3 chicken breast halves, cooked and shredded
    3/4 cup onion, chopped
    1 pound Monterey Jack cheese, shredded
    2 cups sour cream
    1 teaspoon seasoned salt
    seasoned pepper, to taste

Saute onion in oil until tender. Add tomatoes, rice seasoning mix and salsa jalapeña. Simmer 20 minutes; set aside to cool. Pour 1/2 cup sauce in bottom of a 9" x 13" x 2" baking dish. Arrange a layer of tortillas over sauce. Top with 1/3 of sauce, chicken, onion and cheese. Repeat twice (3 layers). Combine sour cream and seasoned salt. Spread over casserole to edges of dish. Sprinkle lightly with seasoned pepper. Bake at 325 degrees for 30 minutes. To serve, cut into squares.

Carol Kagy   **Norwalk High School, Norwalk, CA**

Southwest Chicken Spaghetti

Serves 10

    1 (12 ounce) package vermicelli
    1 medium onion, chopped
    1 bell pepper, chopped
    1 (10 ounce) can Ro-Tel (diced tomatoes and green chiles)
    1 (13 ounce) can mushroom pieces
    2 (10.5 ounce) cans cream of chicken soup
    2 (10 ounce) cans chunk chicken
    2 cups cheddar cheese, shredded

Cook vermicelli as suggested; set aside. In a large skillet, saute onion and bell pepper. Stir in Rotel, mushrooms, soup and chicken. Let simmer 10 minutes. In a very large bowl, combine vermicelli, grated cheese and simmered mixture. Place all ingredients in a large casserole dish or a 9" x 13" pan. Bake at 350 degrees for 1 hour.

"The Ro-Tel adds the spicy Southwest taste. This is great for a crowd."

Judy Banks   **Temecula Valley High School, Temecula, CA**

Southwest White Chile

Serves 6

> 2 tablespoons olive oil
> 1 1/2 pounds boneless, skinless chicken breasts, cubed
> 1/4 cup onion, chopped
> 2 cups chicken broth
> 1/2 (4 ounce) can green chiles, diced
> 1 teaspoon garlic powder
> 1 teaspoon cumin
> 1 teaspoon oregano
> 1 teaspoon fresh cilantro leaves, chopped
> 1/4 teaspoon red pepper
> 2 (19 ounce) cans white kidney beans, undrained
> *Garnish:* 1 cup Monterey shredded jack cheese, 1/2 cup sliced green onions

Heat oil in 5 quart saucepan over medium heat. Add chicken and cook 4 to 5 minutes, stirring often. Remove chicken with slotted spoon; cover and keep warm. Add onion to saucepan and cook 2 minutes. Stir in broth, green chiles and spices; simmer 30 minutes. Add chicken and beans to broth and heat through. Serve in small bowls with desired garnishes.

"This chili is great served with tortilla chips!"

Jill Marsh   **Warren High School, Downey, CA**

Stacked Chicken Enchiladas

Serves 4

> 2 cups chicken, cooked, shredded
> 1 cup sour cream
> 2 green onions, chopped
> 1/2 teaspoon salt
> 1/4 teaspoon cumin
> 6 corn tortillas
> 1 (10 ounce) can enchilada sauce
> 2 1/2 cups cheddar cheese, shredded

Combine chicken, sour cream, green onions, salt and cumin in mixing bowl; set aside. Dip tortillas in enchilada sauce. Place in a 1 1/2 quart casserole dish, covering the bottom. Top with a layer of filling and sprinkle with a layer of cheese. Repeat. Before adding last layer of cheese, pour remaining enchilada sauce over layers. Finish with cheese. Bake at 350 degrees for 40 minutes.

Debbie Harvey   **Amador Valley High School, Pleasanton, CA**

Swordfish with Salsa

Serves 4

Salsa:
3 large tomatoes, chopped
1 fresh jalapeño, chopped
3 green onions, chopped
2 tablespoons cilantro, chopped
Marinade:
juice from 3 limes
2 tablespoons olive oil
1/4 cup ginger root, peeled, chopped
2 tablespoons cilantro, chopped
1 teaspoon ground pepper
4 swordfish steaks
1 large avocado, peeled, sliced

Prepare salsa by combining tomatoes, jalapeño, green onions and and cilantro in blender; blend, then refrigerate 1 hour. While salsa chills, combine lime juice, olive oil, ginger root, cilantro and ground pepper. Pour marinade over swordfish steaks until coated; cover and marinate 1 hour. Grill steaks approximately 10 minutes. When ready to serve, top each steak with avocado slices and a spoonful of salsa.

Amy Tavaglione-Rudolph   **Etiwanda High School, Etiwanda, CA**

Turkey Burrito Pie

Serves 4

2 tablespoons oil
1 small onion, chopped
1 pound ground turkey or hamburger
1 (16 ounce) can refried beans
1 (7 ounce) can salsa
garlic salt, to taste
1/2 teaspoon cumin seed
2 (12") flour tortillas
1/2 cup black olives, sliced
3 cups jack or cheddar cheese, shredded
Garnish: chopped tomatoes, chopped green onions, sour cream

Saute onions in oil until limp; remove and set aside. Brown ground turkey or beef, breaking up with spoon until browned and crumbled; drain fat. Add onions, beans, salsa, garlic, cumin and olives. Simmer, stirring 4 to 5 minutes. Place one tortilla in a lightly greased 10" pie plate. Cover with half of the meat mixture, then half of the cheese. Repeat. Bake at 350 degrees for 30 minutes. Remove from oven and garnish as desired.

"A fun, quick dinner everyone will enjoy. Serve with a green salad."
Beverly Fincher-Ranger   **Carpinteria High School, Carpinteria, CA**

Turkey Tamale Pie

Serves 6

    1 pound ground turkey
    2 cloves garlic, minced, divided
    1 large onion, chopped
    1 (14 ounce) can tomatoes
    1 (14 ounce) can corn, drained
    1 (14 ounce) can olives, drained
    1 cup corn meal
    1 1/2 tablespoons chili powder
    1 teaspoon cumin
    1 teaspoon salt
    1 egg, beaten
    1 cup milk
    2 cups cheese, shredded

Brown ground turkey with 1 clove garlic and onion; drain fat. Add remaining ingredients except cheese and simmer 5 to 10 minutes. Pour into greased baking dish. Cover with shredded cheese and bake at 350 degrees for 45 minutes.

"My grandmother made this for years. It has been a family favorite."

Jeri Lundy   **Grossmont High School, La Mesa, CA**

Viva La Chicken

Serves 12

    6 chicken breast halves, cooked
    12 tortillas
    1 can cream of chicken soup
    1 cup milk
    3/4 cup onion
    1 (7 ounce) can salsa
    2 cups cheddar cheese, shredded

Cut chicken and tortillas into strips. Combine soup, milk, onion and salsa. Layer tortillas, chicken, soup mixture and cheese in a buttered baking dish. Refrigerate 24 hours. Bake at 300 degrees for 1 1/2 hours.

Debbie L. Rothe   **Alta Loma High School, Alta Loma, CA**

White Chicken Enchiladas

Serves 12

    1 (3 to 3-1/2 pound) chicken, cooked, deboned, shredded
    1 (4 ounce) can green chiles, diced
    2 cups sour cream
    2 (10.75 ounce) cans cream of chicken soup
    1 (4 ounce) can black olives, sliced
    1 pound Monterey Jack or cheddar cheese, shredded
    12 flour tortillas

Cut chicken into bite-sized pieces; set aside. Mix together chiles, sour cream, soup, olives and half of the cheese; divide mixture in half. To half of the mixture, add chicken. Spoon this mixture down center of each tortilla and roll up, placing seam side down in a 9" x 13" greased pan. Cover tortillas with remaining half of mixture. Top with remaining cheese and bake at 350 degrees for 30 to 45 minutes, until heated through.

"Delicious enchilada recipe from Bonnie Blank, one of our school counselors."

Marty Parker   **Poway High School, Poway, CA**
Linda Woolley   **Redlands High School, Redlands, CA**

Aztec Tacos

Makes 6

> 1 to 2 tablespoons butter
> 12 corn tortillas
> $1/2$ to 1 cup cheese, shredded
> 6 slices turkey or ham
> *Garnish:* salsa, guacamole, sour cream

Butter one side of tortilla. Place one tortilla, buttered side down in a skillet. Sprinkle with cheese, top with a slice of ham, then sprinkle with more cheese. Place a buttered tortilla on top; butter side up. Fry 1 to 2 minutes on each side. Repeat for remaining tacos. Cut into fourths and serve plain or with salsa, guacamole or sour cream. Note: You can also add green chiles with cheese. Spray tortilla with nonstick cooking spray instead of butter.

"This is a quick, easy recipe that kids love."

Kathy Sandoz   **Mesa Junior High School, Mesa, AZ**

Black Bean Tacos

Serves 6

Beans:
1 cup dried black beans
4 cups water, for soaking beans
1 tablespoon salad oil
1 large onion, chopped
1 clove garlic
1 small dried hot red chile, crushed
$1/2$ teaspoon salt
2 $1/2$ cups water

Tacos:
1 head romaine lettuce, shredded
1 large tomato, chopped
1 large red bell pepper, cut into thin strips
6 green onions, thinly sliced (including tops)
$1/4$ cup red wine vinegar
1 large clove garlic, minced or pressed
1 teaspoon chili powder
$1/2$ teaspoon ground cumin
$1/2$ teaspoon salt
$1/4$ teaspoon pepper
2 tablespoons salad oil
12 (7" to 9") flour tortillas
$1/4$ cup extra sharp cheddar cheese, shredded
1 cup plain nonfat yogurt
sliced black olives (optional)

Prepare black beans: rinse beans well. In a 3 to 4 quart pan, bring water to a boil over high heat; add beans, cook 2 minutes. Remove from heat; cover and let stand 1 hour; drain and rinse. Heat 1 tablespoon salad oil in pan over medium heat. Add chopped onion and cook, stirring occasionally, until limp, about 20 minutes. Add beans, garlic, dried hot red chile, salt and remaining water. Bring to a boil over high heat; reduce heat, cover and simmer until beans are tender and liquid is absorbed, about 2 hours. Meanwhile, place lettuce, tomato, bell pepper and green onions in a large bowl, In a small bowl, stir together vinegar, garlic, chili powder, cumin, salt and pepper. Add oil and whisk until blended. Pour over vegetables and toss well. Stack tortillas, wrap in foil and place in 350 degree oven until hot, about 15 minutes. Spoon about 1/4 cup of the bean mixture into each tortilla; add about 1/2 cup lettuce mixture, 1 teaspoon cheddar cheese and 1 1/3 tablespoons yogurt. Sprinkle with olives, if desired. Fold tortilla over filling.

"This is a great recipe–my 13-year old daughter loves these!"

Debbie Grove   **Piner High School, Santa Rosa, CA**

Breakfast Burritos

Serves 1

    2 flour tortillas
    1 large potato, boiled
    2 teaspoons oil
    2 teaspoons green chile, diced
    1/4 cup cheddar cheese, shredded

Wrap tortillas in foil and warm in oven at 300 degrees for 10 minutes. Dice potato and brown in skillet with oil. Stir in chiles and cheese. Fill tortillas with mixture and enjoy.

"My family loves these. They are quick, easy and delicious."

Carol Jones   **Pierce High School, Arbuckle, CA**

Cheese & Vegetable Tacos

Serves 5

    1 (8.5 ounce) package flour tortillas
    2 tablespoons oil
    2 cups broccoli florets
    1 cup fresh mushrooms, sliced
    1 cup red bell pepper, diced
    1/2 cup green onion, sliced
    1 1/2 cups cheddar cheese, shredded

Preheat oven to 350 degrees. Wrap tortillas tightly in foil. Bake for 10 minutes or until softened; remove from oven. Increase oven temperature to 400 degrees. Meanwhile, heat oil in large skillet over high heat. Add vegetables and stir fry 2 to 3 minutes or until tender-crisp; cool slightly. Stir in cheese. Place 1/3 cup filling down center of each tortilla; fold in half or roll. Place on ungreased cookie sheet. Bake 5 minutes. Serve immediately.

"Top with salsa, serve with refried beans From the Pillsbury Shortcut Cookbook"

Maridel Anagnos   **Tokay High School, Lodi, CA**

Chilaquiles

Serves 5

       3 chiles, halved and seeded
       7 green tomatillos
       3 cloves garlic
       2 tablespoons ground cumin
       4 sprigs cilantro
       2 cups chicken stock
       24 corn tortillas, cut in strips
       1/2 head lettuce, shredded
       1 whole lemon, cut in wedges
       Parmesan cheese, grated

Boil chiles and tomatillos in water until skins are soft, being careful not to overcook. Remove from heat, allow to cool slightly; peel tomatillos and finely chop. In a blender, combine tomatillos, chiles, garlic, cumin and cilantro with chicken stock. Blend for 30 seconds until well blended, making a green sauce. Put sauce in large skillet and simmer for 10 to 15 minutes. Add tortilla strips to sauce and simmer until tortillas have dissolved into the sauce. Mix in lettuce and squeeze on some lemon. Top with Parmesan cheese.

"One of my students, Liliana Cantoran, prepared this authentic Mexican favorite for our class. Serve with Spanish rice and beans."

Beth Gonzalez   **Bolsa Grande High School, Garden Grove, CA**

Chile Egg Puff

Serves 6

       10 eggs
       1/2 cup flour
       1 teaspoon baking powder
       1/2 teaspoon salt
       1/2 cup margarine, melted
       1 pint small curd cottage cheese
       1 pound jack cheese, shredded
       1 small can green chiles, diced

Beat eggs with electric mixer until light and lemon in color. Add flour, baking powder and salt. Beat in margarine, cottage cheese and jack cheese. Stir in chiles. Pour into buttered 9" x 13" pan. Bake at 350 degrees for 35 minutes or until firm and lightly browned on top.

Anne Bengtson   **Morse High School, San Diego, CA**

Chile Relleno Casserole

Serves 6

    6 to 8 large fresh green chiles
    4 eggs, beaten
    2 teaspoons cumin powder
    $1/2$ teaspoon salt
    $1/2$ teaspoon pepper
    3 cups jack cheese, shredded

Place chiles on a broiler pan and broil, turning frequently to blister skin. Remove from broiler, place a in plastic bag for 5 minutes, then remove skin. Slice chiles lengthwise, remove seeds and lay in oblong pan. In bowl, combine eggs, cumin, salt and pepper. Cover chiles with cheese and pour egg mixture over top. Bake at 350 degrees for 25 minutes, or until eggs are set and cheese is melted.

"My student, Bree Robbins, got this recipe from her grandma
and she says even her dad likes it!"

Linda Silvasy　　　　　　　　　　　**Olive Peirce Middle School, Ramona, CA**

Daddy's Eggs

Serves 4

    $1/2$ cup vegetable oil
    3 to 4 corn tortillas, diced into small pieces
    $1/2$ cup onion, diced
    1 clove garlic, minced
    1 to 2 tomatoes, seeded, diced
    6 eggs, well beaten
    2 cups cooked rice, preferably leftover Mexican rice, or white rice
    $1/2$ cup Ortega Green Chile Salsa
    salt and pepper, to taste

In large nonstick skillet, heat $1/4$ cup vegetable oil. Fry corn tortilla pieces until very crisp. Remove and drain; set aside. In small skillet saute onion, garlic and tomatoes until onion is clear and tender. Remove and set aside. In same skillet, scramble eggs until just done; don't overcook. Remove eggs and set aside. Heat remaining oil in skillet and fry rice until well heated and slightly crisp. Add tortilla pieces, onion, garlic and tomatoes, eggs and salsa. Heat through. Season to taste with salt and pepper. Serve immediately.

"My husband created this dish when we were first married, and it has become a
family favorite. It is also a great way to use leftovers from other Mexican meals."

Pam Bonilla　　　　　　　　**San Gorgonio High School, San Bernardino, CA**

Eggs and Cheese
Serves 4

- 1/4 cup vegetable oil
- 1 medium yellow onion, peeled, finely chopped
- 1 medium sweet green pepper, cored, seeded, finely chopped
- 3 medium tomatoes, peeled and chopped or 1 (16 ounce) can tomatoes, drained, chopped
- 1 whole canned jalapeño pepper, rinsed, seeded, chopped
  or 1/4 teaspoon crushed red pepper
- 2 cloves garlic, peeled, minced
- 1/2 teaspoon salt
- 1/2 teaspoon ground cumin
- 2 teaspoons chili powder
- 1/4 teaspoon dried oregano, crumbled
- 4 corn tortillas
- 4 eggs
- 1 cup Monterey Jack cheese, shredded

Preheat broiler. Heat 2 tablespoons oil in heavy 2 quart saucepan over moderate heat. Add onion and green pepper and cook, uncovered for 5 minutes, or until onion is soft. Raise heat to moderately high. Add tomatoes, jalapeño pepper, garlic and salt and cook, uncovered, for 5 minutes, or until slightly thickened. Stir in cumin, chili powder and oregano and remove sauce from heat. While sauce is cooking, arrange tortillas on ungreased baking sheet. About 2 minutes before sauce is done, heat remaining 2 tablespoons oil in a heavy 12" skillet over moderate heat. Break eggs into skillet, spacing them so they don't overlap. Lower heat slightly and cook, uncovered, for 1 minute, or until the whites are set. Using a pancake turner, carefully remove eggs from skillet and place on each tortilla. Pour sauce over eggs, sprinkle with cheese and place under broiler for 1 minute.

"If you want to get a head start on this dish, make the sauce in advance, then reheat it while eggs are cooking."

Kevin Moretti   **Chico Junior High School, Chico, CA**

Goooood Chili Rellenos
Serves 6

- nonstick cooking spray
- 3 (7 ounce) cans green chiles, diced
- 2 1/2 to 3 cups jack cheese, shredded
- 2 1/2 to 3 cups cheddar cheese, shredded
- 1 1/2 small cans evaporated milk
- 4 1/2 tablespoons flour
- 5 eggs
- 1 (8 ounce) can tomato sauce

Lightly spray bottom of 9" x 13" oblong pan with nonstick cooking spray. Generously layer green chiles, jack cheese and cheddar cheese, repeating until dish is almost full (reserving enough shredded cheese for garnish). Mix milk, flour and eggs with electric mixer. Pour egg mixture evenly over chile/cheese layers. Bake at 350

Southwest Tortellini Chowder
Try this with the cheese muffins!
Page 44

Smokey Cheese Chile Muffins
Not just for breakfast!
Page 60

Chili Burrito Cups
These work as a
side dish or entreé!
Page 80

degrees for 30 minutes. Remove from oven and pour tomato sauce evenly over top; sprinkle with remaining cheese. Bake an additional 15 minutes.

"Oh, so good!! Thanks to Doris from D.O. for a great recipe!"

Marilyn Bankhead   **San Marcos High School, San Marcos, CA**

Huevos Rancheros

Serves 6

    2 tablespoons vegetable oil
    1 small onion, chopped
    1 green pepper, chopped
    1 (8 ounce) can tomato sauce
    1/2 cup water
    1 tomato, chopped
    1 clove garlic, minced
    1 teaspoon oregano
    1/2 teaspoon salt
    1 teaspoon hot pepper sauce
    6 eggs
    corn tortillas

In a large skillet, saute onion and green pepper in oil. Add tomato sauce, water, tomato, garlic, oregano, salt and pepper sauce. Cover and simmer about 20 minutes. Break eggs, one at a time, into sauce. Cover and simmer 5 minutes, or until eggs are set. Dip tortillas in sauce, serve each egg on top of tortilla with sauce on top.

"Serve these with refried beans."

Monica Blanchette   **Landmark Middle School, Moreno Valley, CA**

Lowfat Chile Cheese Casserole

Serves 4 - 6

    1 cup long grain rice
    1 can green chiles, whole, seeded, diced
    1 1/3 cups light or nonfat sour cream
    1/4 pound reduced fat jack cheese, shredded
    1/4 pound mozzarella cheese, shredded
    1/4 teaspoon beau monde
    garlic powder, to taste
    1/2 teaspoon garlic salt
    salt and pepper, to taste

Prepare rice according to package directions. In a greased 1 1/2 quart casserole dish, combine cooked rice with chiles, sour cream, 1 1/2 cups cheeses, beau monde, garlic powder, garlic salt and salt and pepper. Sprinkle remaining cheese over top and bake, uncovered at 350 degrees for 30 minutes, until cheese is bubbly and rice is heated through.

*"If you don't like garlic, you may omit it, but it is a little bland without it.
This is a quick and easy meal to make."*

Karen Peters   **Vaca Peña Middle School, Vacaville, CA**

Meatless Sour Cream Enchiladas

Serves 6

    1 (10 ounce) can enchilada sauce
    1 (16 ounce) can whole tomatoes
    1/3 cup onion, chopped
    1/2 teaspoon salt
    1/4 cup cooking oil
    12 corn tortillas
    1 1/2 cups cheddar cheese, shredded
    1 1/2 cups sour cream

In large saucepan, combine enchilada sauce, tomatoes, onion and salt; heat to boiling, stirring frequently to break up tomatoes. Lower heat and simmer. Heat oil over medium-high heat. Dip tortillas in hot oil for several seconds, then drain. Continue until all tortillas have been softened. On each tortilla, place a heaping tablespoon of sauce and sprinkle with cheese. Roll up and place, seam side down, in a shallow baking dish. Pour remaining sauce over enchiladas and sprinkle with remaining cheese. Bake at 400 degrees for 15 minutes. Spoon sour cream over enchiladas and serve hot.

Ava Smalley   **La Puente High School, La Puente, CA**

Meatless Tex-Mex Lasagna

Serves 6

    1 (30 ounce) can refried beans
    1 (16 ounce) jar mild chunky salsa
    1 (11 ounce) can whole kernel corn, drained
    1 (4 ounce) can green chiles, diced
    3 cups cheddar cheese, shredded
    1 (15 ounce) carton ricotta cheese
    1 (8 ounce) package lasagna noodles, cooked

Prepare noodles according to package directions. In large bowl, combine first 4 ingredients. In another bowl, combine cheeses. Spread 1 cup bean mixture in bottom of a 13" x 9" x 2" baking dish. Layer half of noodles, half of bean mixture and 1/4 of cheese mixture. Repeat, starting with noodles and ending with cheese mixture. Bake at 350 degrees for 45 minutes to 1 hour.

"Nice change from lasagna–great as microwaved leftovers."

Merideth Marcus   **San Pasqual High School, Escondido, CA**

Mex-Tex Impossible Green Chile Pie

Serves 6

    2 (4 ounce) cans green chiles, diced, drained
    4 cups cheddar cheese, shredded
    2 cups milk
    1 cup biscuit mix
    4 eggs

Heat oven to 425 degrees. Grease a large pie plate. Sprinkle chiles and cheese in plate. Beat remaining ingredients until smooth; pour into pan over chiles and cheese. Bake for 25 to 30 minutes, until a knife inserted in center comes out clean. Let stand 10 mintues before cutting.

"Serve with sour cream or guacamole. This is quick, easy and fun!"

Anita Huckert   **McKee Middle School, Bakersfield, CA**

Mexican Oven Omelet

Serves 6 - 8

     8 eggs, beaten
     1 1/2 cups milk
     1 teaspoon garlic salt
     1 tomato, chopped
     1 (7 ounce) can green chiles, diced
     1/4 cup green onion, chopped
     2 tablespoons cilantro, chopped
     8 ounces jack cheese, shredded
     Garnish: salsa, sour cream

Combine eggs, milk and garlic salt. Stir in tomato, chiles, green onion, cilantro and cheese. Pour into greased 1-1/2 quart shallow casserole. Bake at 350 degrees for 40 minutes. Serve with garnishes.

Lucille Bell   **Quartz Hill High School, Quartz Hill, CA**

No-Meat Taco Casserole

Serves 8

     1 medium onion, chopped
     2 tablespoons salad oil
     1 (1 pound, 12 ounce) can tomatoes
     1 package Lawry's Taco Mix
     1/2 teaspoon Lawry's Seasoned Salt
     1 (4 ounce) can green chiles, chopped
     1 (6 ounce) package tortilla chips
     1 pound jack cheese, shredded
     1 cup sour cream
     1/2 cup cheddar cheese, shredded
     Garnish: chopped black olives, salsa, chopped green onions, cilantro,
          tomato wedges

Saute onion in oil until tender. Add canned tomatoes, taco seasoning, seasoned salt and chiles. Simmer, uncovered 10 to 15 minutes. Butter or grease bottom and sides of a 2 quart, deep casserole dish. Layer dish with 1/2 of the tortilla chips, half tomato sauce and 1/2 jack cheese. Repeat layers. Top with sour cream. Bake 30 minutes at 325 degrees. Sprinkle with cheddar cheese and bake an additional 10 minutes. Let stand 10 minutes before serving. Garnish with desired toppings.

"Gets great reviews. Prepare ahead and pop in the oven for easy entertaining. Add a garden salad, beans and rice, and you have a complete fiesta. Just say "Ole'!"

Barbara Allen   **Ayala High School, Chino Hills, CA**

Spinach Broccoli Enchiladas

Serves 4

    1 tablespoon olive oil
    1 onion, chopped
    1 1/2 cups cooked spinach, drained, chopped
    1 cup cheddar cheese, shredded
    8 ounces lowfat ricotta cheese
    1 cup broccoli, cooked, drained, chopped
    1 1/4 cups salsa
    3/4 teaspoon ground cumin
    1/4 teaspoon garlic powder
    8 (6" to 7") flour tortillas

Heat olive oil in a large skillet over medium-high heat; add onion and saute until tender. Add spinach, cooking and stirring until any moisture evaporates. Remove from heat and stir in 1/2 cup cheddar cheese, all the ricotta cheese, broccoli, 1/2 cup salsa, cumin and garlic powder. Divide mixture evenly among tortillas, spooning it down the center of each one. Roll tortillas and place, seam side down in lightly greased 11" x 7" x 2" microwave safe baking dish. Spoon remaining salsa evenly over enchiladas. Cover with plastic wrap, leaving a corner uncovered for venting. Microwave on HIGH for 10 minutes, rotating dish 1/4 turn every 4 minutes. CAREFULLY remove plastic wrap and check that enchiladas are heated through. Sprinkle remaining cheese over top and microwave just until cheese melts.

Gloria King　　　　　　　　　　**Schurr High School, Montebello, CA**

Spinach Enchiladas

Serves 6

    1 (10 ounce) package frozen chopped spinach, thawed, pressed dry
    1 (10.75) ounce can cream of chicken soup
    1 (8 ounce) carton sour cream
    1 (4 ounce) can green chiles, diced
    2 tablespoons green onion, minced
    12 (4 1/2") corn tortillas
    vegetable oil
    4 cups Monterey Jack cheese, shredded, divided
    3/4 cup onion, minced
    nonstick cooking spray

Using a blender or food processor, combine first 5 ingredients until smooth; set aside. Fry tortillas, one at a time, in 1/4" of hot oil for about 5 seconds on each side or until softened. Drain tortillas well on paper towels. Fill each tortilla with 1 tablespoon cheese and 1 tablespoon onion; roll up and place, seam side down, in a 12" x 8" x 2" baking dish that has been sprayed with nonstick cooking spray. Spoon spinach mixture over tortillas. Sprinkle with remaining cheese. Bake, uncovered, at 325 degrees for 30 minutes. Serve immediately.

"An excellent Mexican dish for vegetable eaters."

Judy Dobkins　　　　　　　　**Redlands High School, Redlands, CA**

Three-Way Spicy Vegetable Filling

Makes 5 - 6

2 tablespoons salad oil
1 large onion, chopped
2 large carrots, thinly sliced
1 clove garlic, minced or pressed
2 1/2 teaspoons chili powder
1 teaspoon salt
3/4 teaspoon ground cumin
3/4 teaspoon oregano leaves
4 (medium-sized) zucchini, cut into 1/2" cubes
1 (large) green or red bell pepper, seeded and chopped
1 (8 ounce) can whole kernel corn, drained
1 (16 ounce) can kidney beans, drained

In large frying pan, over medium-high heat, heat oil. Add onion, carrots, garlic, chili powder, salt, cumin and oregano. Cook stirring constantly until onion is limp, about 10 minutes. Stir in zucchini, bell pepper, corn and beans, cook, stirring often, until zucchini is tender crisp, 7 to 8 minutes. Spoon into a serving dish and serve hot. Use as a filling for tacos, tostadas or burritos.

"A great vegetarian meal! One of our summer favorites!"

Kris Hawkins   **Clovis West High School, Fresno, CA**

DESSERTS

Almond Flan

Serves 8

  1/2 cup sugar
  1 2/3 cups sweetened condensed milk
  1 cup milk
  3 eggs
  3 egg yolks
  1 teaspoon vanilla extract
  1 cup slivered almonds, coarsely ground

Sprinkle sugar evenly in a 9" cake pan and place over medium heat. Using oven mitts, caramelize sugar by shaking the pan occasionally until sugar is melted and has turned a golden brown. Allow to cool. (Mixture may crack slightly.) Blend remaining ingredients at high speed for 15 seconds. Pour over caramelized sugar. Cover pan with aluminum foil and place in a larger, shallow pan containing 1" of hot water. Bake at 350 degrees for 55 minutes or until a knife inserted in center comes out clean. Remove pan from water and uncover. Let it cool on a wire rack at least 30 minutes. Loosen edge with a spatula. Place a serving plate upside down on top of the cake pan and quickly invert flan onto it.

"This flan will keep in the pan up to a week in the refrigerator.
It is silky smooth. The almonds rise to the top so that when you turn it,
you have an almond crust. Easy and elegant."

Alice Lewandowski   **Linden High School, Linden, CA**

Apple Cinnamon Tortilla Strips
Serves 6

nonstick cooking spray
1 tablespoon sugar
1/4 teaspoon cinnamon
4 (6") lowfat flour tortillas, cut in 1/4" strips
2 tablespoons apple jelly, melted

Preheat oven 350 degrees. Coat cookie sheet with nonstick spray. Combine sugar and cinnamon in small bowl. In large bowl, toss tortilla strips with melted apple jelly. Sprinkle strips with sugar-cinnamon mixture. Toss. Spread strips on cookie sheet in SINGLE LAYER. Bake 20 minutes, tossing every 7 minutes, until golden.

"This is a good alternative to high fat desserts and chips."

Nancie Wilson   **Woodland High School, Woodland, CA**

Apple Fritters
Serves 6

2 to 3 pippin apples
2 cups flour
3 teaspoons baking powder
1 teaspoon sugar
1/8 teaspoon salt
1 1/4 cups milk
3 tablespoons salad oil
3 egg whites
salad oil for deep frying
maple syrup

Peel and core apples; slice into 1/4-inch thick pieces. Sift flour, measure, and sift into mixing bowl with baking powder, sugar, and salt. Combine milk and oil, and stir into sifted dry ingredients. Beat egg whites until stiff but not dry, and fold into flour mixture. Allow to stand before dipping fruit. Drain prepared fruit well on paper toweling. Gently fold fruit into batter. Using two large spoons, scoop batter to from one large ball and carefully lower into heated oil (375 degrees). Fry until golden brown; drain. Drizzle fritter with syrup and serve at once.

"One of our favorite Mexican restaurants is known for serving apple fritters prior to the meal. They are also delicious when prepared with pineapples or bananas."

Gerry Henderson   **Temple City High School, Temple, CA**

Berry Good Sundaes
Serves 4

    4 (6") flour tortillas
    1 1/2 cups nectarines, peeled, diced
    1 1/2 cups strawberries or raspberries, chopped
    2 tablespoons sugar
    1/2 teaspoon grated lemon peel
    4 (3 ounce) scoops vanilla ice cream
    fresh mint sprigs

Preheat oven to 350 degrees. Soften tortillas in microwave for 30 seconds. Press each tortilla down into ungreased 10 ounce custard cup. Bake 10 to 15 minutes, or until crisp; set aside to cool. Combine nectarines, berries, sugar and lemon peel in large bowl; mix gently until well blended. To assemble, remove tortillas from custard cups. Place each tortilla shell on dessert plate and fill with ice cream. Spool equal portions of fruit mixture over tops. Garnish with mint sprigs.

Angela Cruz-Trujillo   **Valley View High School, Moreno Valley, CA**

Bread Pudding (Capirotada)
Serves 6

    1 loaf day old white bread, cubed
    1 1/4 cups water
    1 cup dark brown sugar
    6 tablespoons butter or margarine
    1 cup raisins
    1 cup unsalted peanuts
    1/2 cup mild cheddar cheese, shredded

If bread is fresh, toast before cutting into cubes. Heat water in a saucepan, add sugar and butter; stir until dissolved. Add bread pieces to liquid and soak completely. Add raisins, peanuts and cheese. Pour into a buttered 8" x 8" pan and cover. Bake at 325 degrees for 15 minutes. Remove from oven and cool.

"My husband is especially fond of this dessert.
His mother and grandmother often made this for family gatherings."

Wanda Shelton   **Newport Harbor High School, Newport Beach, CA**

Buñuelos
Makes 36

    1 egg
    2 cups water
    2 1/2 cups flour
    oil, for frying
    1/4 cup sugar
    4 tablespoons cinnamon
    Cookie Fryer or Rosette Irons
    1/4 cup sugar
    3 tablespoons cinnamon

Mix egg, water and flour in order given, in blender until it resembles cream. Heat oil to 375 degrees. Heat cookie frying irons in oil. Slip hot irons into oil and then into batter until 3/4 covered (important!). Place irons in hot oil and fry each until it slips off. Fry only a few at a time. Drain; sprinkle with sugar and cinnamon.

"From my family in Santa Fe, New Mexico.
It's a very old recipe used in many fiestas!"

Elizabeth Ward   **Hesperia High School, Hesperia, CA**

Chocolate Cheesecake con Cafe

Serves 10

Crust:
9 ounce box chocolate wafers, broken
2 tablespoons sugar
2 teaspoons instant espresso powder
3 ounces semi-sweet chocolate, chopped
6 tablespoons unsalted butter, melted
Filling:
4 (8 ounce) packages cream cheese, softened
1 1/4 cups sugar
1/4 cup coffee liqueur
3 tablespoons instant espresso powder
1 tablespoon vanilla
4 large eggs
6 ounces semi-sweet chocolate, chopped
Topping:
1 1/4 cups sour cream
3 tablespoons sugar
2 teaspoons instant espresso powder

Crust: Grind wafers, sugar and powder in food processor. Add chocolate and butter until moist crumbs form. Press on to bottom and sides of 9" springform pan; set aside. Prepare filling: preheat oven to 350 degrees. In mixer, blend together cream cheese and sugar. In saucepan over low heat, combine coffee liqueur and espresso powder until blended. Stir in vanilla; add to cream cheese mixture. Add eggs, one at a time. Pour filling into 2 bowls, dividing evenly. Pour one bowlful into pie crust and bake about 25 minutes, until partially set. Melt chocolate and add to remaining bowl. Carefully spoon chocolate filling over pie and bake about 30 minutes longer, until set on sides. Cool 20 minutes. Prepare topping: mix sour cream, sugar and espresso powder. Pour over cheesecake. Bake additional 10 minutes. Cool and refrigerate before serving.

Betty Wells   **Oroville High School, Oroville, CA**

Cinnamon Oranges

Serves 4

> 3 oranges, peeled, thinly sliced crosswise
> 1/4 cup sugar
> 1/4 teaspoon ground cinnamon

Place sliced oranges in a serving bowl. Mix sugar and cinnamon together in a small bowl; sprinkle over oranges. Cover bowl and refrigerate at least one hour.

"Approximately 100 calories per serving. Excellent!"

Denise Stallman   **Rancho Bernardo High School, San Diego, CA**

Cinnamon Tostada Sundae

Serves 1

> 1 (8") flour tortilla
> 1/2 teaspoon cinnamon
> 1 teaspoon sugar
> 1 to 2 scoops vanilla ice cream
> hot fudge or chocolate syrup
> *Garnish:* colored candy sprinkles, maraschino cherries

Deep fry tortilla in the shape of a bowl, drain, upside down on paper towels. While still hot, dust inside and outside of tortilla with a mixture of cinnamon and sugar. Place a scoop or two of vanilla ice cream in tortilla bowl; top with hot fudge or syrup. Garnish with candy sprinkles and a cherry. Serve immediately.

"My mom and I created this dessert to be served at my dad's retirement party."

Gail Marlow-Dickey   **Montclair High School, Montclair, CA**

Fiesta Cake

Serves 8 - 12

> 1/ cup butter, softened
> 1 1/2 cups sugar
> 2 eggs
> 1 teaspoon vanilla
> 1 cup bananas, mashed
> 1 small can pineapple, crushed, drained
> 2 cups flour, sifted
> 1/2 teaspoon salt
> 1 teaspoon each baking soda and baking powder
> 1/2 cup buttermilk
> *Garnish:* maraschino cherries, whipped cream

Cream butter and sugar in large mixing bowl. Blend in eggs, vanilla, mashed bananas and drained pineapple. Sift dry ingredients into creamed mixture alternately with buttermilk; mix well. Pour into a greased and floured 9" x 13" cake pan. Bake at 375 degrees for 25 minutes. Cool completely. Garnish with cherries and whipped cream.

Susan Lefler   **Ramona Junior High School, Chino, CA**

Flan

Serves 6

1/3 cup sugar
6 eggs
6 tablespoons sugar
2 cups milk
1 teaspoon vanilla

Make a hot water bath for the Flan: set a 9" x 1 1/4" pie pan in a slightly larger pan. Fill the outer pan with just enough hot tap water to come up around the other pan; hold down the pie pan so it won't float. Then remove the pie pan and put only the pan of water in a preheating 350 degree oven while you mix the Flan. In small frying pan over moderate heat, melt sugar, shaking pan instead of stirring. Once melted, sugar will caramelize quickly; as soon as it does, pour at once into the 9" pie pan. Using hot pads to protect hands, tilt pan quickly to let syrup flow over bottom and slightly up sides. If syrup hardens before you finish, set pan on moderate heat until syrup softens, then continue. In a bowl, beat together eggs and sugar; add milk and vanilla. Set caramel-lined pan in hot water in oven; pour in egg mixture. Bake at 350 degrees for about 25 minutes. Test doneness by pushing Flan in center with back of spoon–when done, a crevice about 3/8" deep forms. Remove from hot water and chill at once. As Flan cools, caramel dissolves somewhat. When cold, loosen just the custard edge, then cover with rimmed serving plate. Holding plate in place, quickly invert. The Flan will slowly slip free and the caramel sauce flows out. Cut in wedges, spoon on sauce. Note: 10 small custard cups may be used instead of pie plate.

"Many students had never sampled flan. It is now a favorite for the holidays."
Ramona Anderson **Mira Mesa High School, San Diego, CA**

Flower Pots Kahlua

Makes 24

24 (new) small, terra cotta flower pots
1 half gallon chocolate almond ice cream, softened
1 half gallon coffee ice cream, softened
24 tablespoons kahlua liqueur (optional)
24 small fresh or silk flowers, such as roses or daisies
1 package Famous Chocolate Wafers, finely crumbled

Fill flower pots half way with chocolate almond ice cream. Fill almost to top with coffee ice cream. Top with 1 tablespoon kahlua (if desired). Sprinkle with chocolate wafer crumbs, covering top. Freeze immediately. (If you work quickly enough, ice cream will not melt enough to be a problem.) *To Serve:* stick a perky flower in the top of the pot, about 1" down into ice cream; place on a small saucer and serve with great drama!

"Guests may be fooled at first and refuse to believe you have given them something edible. That's the fun!"
Helen Lievre **La Cañada High School, La Cañada, CA**

Fried Fruit Burritos

Serves 6 - 8

    1 package dried fruit bits
    $1/2$ cup apple juice
    1 tablespoon cornstarch
    $1/2$ teaspoon cinnamon
    La Tapatia fruit tortillas
    oil, for frying
    powdered sugar

In a small saucepan, combine dried fruit bits, apple juice, cornstarch and cinnamon; cook on medium heat stirring until thickened. Heat 2" oil in skillet on medium-high heat. Spoon 1 heaping tablespoon filling into center of tortilla; roll tightly. Fry in hot oil, turning once, until lightly browned; drain on paper towels. Sprinkle with powdered sugar.

"This is a real treat!"

Jeanne Heinrichs-Suhr　　　　　　　　　　　**Fowler High School, Fowler, CA**

Fried Mexican Ice Cream

Serves 4

    1 pint vanilla ice cream
    $1/2$ cup cornflakes, crushed
    1 teaspoon cinnamon
    2 teaspoons sugar
    1 egg
    oil, for deep frying
    Garnish: honey, whipped cream

Scoop 4 balls of ice cream and place on pie plate; freeze. Mix cornflake crumbs, cinnamon and sugar. Roll frozen ice cream balls in half the crumb mixture and freeze again (about $1/2$ hour). Beat egg; dip coated balls in egg, then roll again in remaining cornflake crumbs. Freeze until ready to use. (For thicker coating, repeat dipping in egg and rolling in crumbs. Heat oil in deep fryer to 350 degrees. Place frozen ice cream balls, one at a time, in basket or on perforated spoon and lower into hot oil for 1 minute. Immediately remove and place in dessert glass. Drizzle with honey and top with a dollop of whipped cream. Balls will be crunchy on the outside and just beginning to melt on the inside.

"To die for!"

Charla Rayl　　　　　　　　　　　**Fallbrook High School, Fallbrook, CA**

Meringues de Chocolate (Chocolate Meringues)

Makes 12

    4 egg whites
    1 cup sugar
    2 tablespoons cocoa
    1 tablespoon water
    $1/2$ teaspoon vanilla

Preheat oven to 225 degrees. Line a baking sheet with parchment paper. Beat egg whites until stiff. Add sugar, a little at a time and continue to beat until glossy. Dissolve cocoa in water; add vanilla. Fold into egg whites and gently blend. Drop meringue by mounds onto parchment paper. Leave at least 1" between meringues. Place in oven for 1 hour to dry. Turn off oven and remove when cooled.

"When I was 10, a family friend always brought meringue cookies when she visited. Now, my 10 year old likes them, as well as my 14 year old!"

Jeri Lane   **Canyon Springs High School, Moreno Valley, CA**

Mexican Fruit Cake

Serves 8

Cake:
2 cups flour
2 cups sugar
2 eggs
2 teaspoons baking soda
1 (20 ounce) can crushed pineapple
1 cup nuts, chopped
1 teaspoon vanilla
nonstick cooking spray
Frosting:
2 cups powdered sugar
8 ounces cream cheese
1 stick margarine
1 teaspoon vanilla

Stir together cake ingredients until well blended. Pour into a 9" x 13" pan that has been sprayed with nonstick cooking spray. Bake at 350 degrees for 45 minutes. While cake is baking, prepare frosting by combining all frosting ingredients and blending until smooth. When cake is done baking, remove from oven and spread with frosting while cake is still hot.

"Great for pot luck!"

Linda Rosensteel   **Sultana High School, Hesperia, CA**

Mexican Pineapple Cake

Serves 12

2 cups unsifted flour
2 teaspoons baking powder
2 cups sugar
1 (20 ounce) can crushed pineapple, undrained
2 eggs
1 cup nuts, chopped

Preheat oven to 350 degrees. In large mixing bowl, gently stir together all ingredients by hand until well combined. Pour into a greased and floured 13" x 9" pan and bake 35 minutes. Remove from oven and cool.

"Won a 1st place in 1984!"

Marjorie Brown   **Cabrillo High School, Lompoc, CA**

Mexican Sweet Rolls

Serves 7

Sweet Rolls:
2 1/2 cups flour
1 package yeast
3 tablespoons sugar
1/2 teaspoon salt
1/2 cup milk
3 tablespoons butter
1 egg
oil
Streusel Topping:
1 tablespoon + 2 teaspoons butter
1/3 cup flour
1/4 cup sugar
1 egg yolk

Combine flour, yeast, sugar and salt in a bowl. Heat milk to 120 degrees; stir in butter. Slowly add to flour mixture. Beat egg and add to flour, stirring to form a soft dough. Knead 5 to 10 minutes, until smooth and elastic. Let dough rest, covered, for 20 minutes. Meanwhile, make streusel topping: cut butter into flour and sugar; stir in egg yolk and set aside. Punch dough down, then divide into 7 pieces. Shape each piece into a smooth ball and flatten into a 3" circle. Slash top to make shell shape. Brush lightly with oil and top with streusel mixture; patting into dough. Cover and refrigerate 2 to 24 hours. Let stand, covered, 10 minutes before baking. Bake in preheated 375 degree oven for 15 to 20 minutes.

Janet Griffith   **Norco High School, Norco, CA**

Mexican Wedding Cakes

Makes 30

1 cup butter, softened
3/4 cup powdered sugar
2 teaspoons vanilla
1 tablespoon water
2 cups flour
1 cup walnuts, finely chopped
powdered sugar, for coating

In a large bowl, cream butter and 3/4 cup powdered sugar. Stir in vanilla and water. In another bowl, mix flour and nuts together. Add to butter mixture. Shape into small balls. Place on ungreased cookie sheet and bake at 300 degrees for 20 minutes. Remove from oven and roll in powdered sugar while still warm.

Carmen Leonard   **Mission Viejo High School, Mission Viejo, CA**

Mexicana Bread Pudding

Serves 8 - 10

    1 cup raisins
    1 cup orange juice
    3/4 cup brown sugar, firmly packed
    1/2 teaspoon cinnamon
    1/4 teaspoon nutmeg
    1/2 teaspoon orange peel, grated
    5 cups French bread cubes, lightly packed
    2 1/2 cups Monterey Jack cheese, shredded
    1/2 cup nuts, chopped
    sweetened whipped cream or ice cream (optional)

In small saucepan, combine raisins, juice, sugar, spices and orange peel; bring to a boil, stirring frequently. In large bowl, toss bread with raisin mixture. Add 2 cups of the cheese and nuts, toss. Turn into buttered 1 1/2 quart baking dish. Sprinkle remaining cheese on top. Bake in preheated 375 degree oven 15 to 20 minutes, until cheese is melted. Serve warm with whipped cream or ice cream, if desired.

Kathy Croxall   **Fontana High School, Fontana, CA**

Orange Caramel Custard (Flan)

Serves 4 - 6

    1/3 cup sugar + 1/4 cup sugar, divided
    1 orange, peeled and broken into small pieces
    2 eggs
    1 (13 ounce) can evaporated milk
    1 teaspoon vanilla
    dash salt
    1/8 teaspoon orange flavoring (optional)

In small skillet, heat and stir 1/3 cup sugar over medium heat until sugar melts and becomes golden brown. Quickly pour caramelized sugar into a metal 9" pie pan, tilting to coat bottom and sides. Sprinkle orange pieces over caramelized sugar. In bowl, beat eggs, stir in milk, 1/4 cup sugar, vanilla, salt and orange flavoring. Pour into caramel coated pie tin. Set pan inside another baking pan on oven rack. Pour hot water around pie tin to depth of 1/2". Bake at 325 degrees 45 to 50 minutes, or until a knife inserted half way between center and edge comes out clean. Chill. Carefully loosen custard from sides and invert on platter.

"A delightful alternative to regular flan."

Carla Escola   **Ripon High School, Ripon, CA**

Pralines

Makes 24

2 cups sugar
2/3 cup milk
1/3 cup light corn syrup
1/4 teaspoon salt
1/2 teaspoon vanilla
1 cup pecans

Combine sugar, milk, corn syrup and salt in heavy saucepan. Heat to boiling over medium heat, stirring constantly. A candy thermometer inserted should register 238 degrees. Remove pan from heat and let cool to 110 degrees; add vanilla. Beat until mixture begins to thicken. Stir in pecans. Working fast, using soup spoons, drop onto buttered waxed paper into individual patties.

"This recipe is a specialty of my former Spanish teacher, Luz Loza."

Terri Gravison **Las Plumas High School, Oroville, CA**

Queso Fresco Crepes

Serves 6

1 cup flour
pinch salt
1 egg
1 cup milk
1/4 cup water (or more, if needed)
3 tablespoons butter, divided, melted
1/2 cup prickly pear jam or marmalade or apricot jam
vegetable oil, for frying
10 to12 ounces queso fresco, ranchero, farmer or ricotta cheese, crumbled
1/2 cup crema or creme fraiche
Garnish: toasted pine nuts

Combine flour, salt and egg in large bowl, then stir in milk, water and 2 tablespoons butter until batter is smooth and thin. Refrigerate 1 to 2 hours. Remove from refrigerator. (Batter should be consistency of whipped cream or buttermilk. Add more water if batter is too thick.) Warm a 7" or 8" nonstick skillet over medium-high heat; brush with oil. Using a 1/4 cup measure, pour 3 to 4 tablespoons batter into skillet quickly. Swirl batter around to cover pan evenly. Fry until surface is no longer shiny, about 45 seconds. Loosen crepe with a table knife or narrow spatula and flip; cook another 45 seconds, slide out of pan. Preheat oven to 325 degrees. In small saucepan, warm jam with 1 tablespoon butter over low heat until syrupy; keep warm. Spoon about 2 tablespoons cheese and 1/2 teaspoon crema into crepe; fold into quarters. Transfer to ovenproof decorative platter. Repeat until you have 12 filled crepes, then cover with foil. Bake for 10 minutes to warm through. Spoon jam syrup over crepes and top with crema and pine nuts.

"A south of the border version of cheese blintzes."

Stephanie San Sebastian **Central High School, Fresno, CA**

Quick & Easy Buñuelos
Serves 4 - 8

1/4 cup granulated sugar
1/2 tablespoon cinnamon
oil for frying
6 flour tortillas, cut into cubes

Mix sugar and cinnamon together and set aside. Fry tortilla cubes in hot oil until fluffy, approximately one minute on each side. Drain on paper tower for two to three minutes. Dip in sugar mixture and serve warm.

"Quick, easy, and good!"

Gage Hewes   **South Pasadena High School, South Pasadena, CA**

Sopaipillas
Serves 8

1 1/2 cups flour
2 teaspoons baking powder
1/2 teaspoon salt
2 tablespoons shortening
1/2 cup lukewarm water
oil, for deep frying
honey, for serving

Sift flour, baking powder and salt into bowl. Cut in shortening. Stir in water, combining with fork into a ball. On floured board, knead dough until smooth and elastic. Cover and let dough rest 15 minutes. Divide dough in half and roll each half into an 8" circle. Cut circles into wedges. Deep fry, a few at a time in oil heated to 400 degrees, turning frequently; cook about 3 minutes as they puff up and turn golden. Drain on paper towels. Serve warm with honey.

"Bite off a corner and pour honey inside. Yum!"

Kathy Arthur   **La Sierra High School, Riverside, CA**

CONTRIBUTORS

D

E

F

G

Contributors

149

Contributors

INDEX TO RECIPES

Main Dishes
Poultry & Seafood

Meatless Main Dishes

Desserts

Notes

Notes

For additional copies of **this** book,
please use the re-order forms below.

For **other** cookbook titles available,
please visit our website:

www.californiacookbook.com

Please send _____ copy(ies) of *A Taste of Mexico* at **$10.95** ea.
(includes tax and postage). Make check payable to *California Cookbook Company, Inc.*
Mail this form with your check to: **8332 Brush St., Huntington Beach, CA 92647**

Enclosed is my check for _____ book(s) at $10.95 each $_____.

Name _____

Street _____

City _____ State _____ Zip _____

Please send _____ copy(ies) of *A Taste of Mexico* at **$10.95** ea.
(includes tax and postage). Make check payable to *California Cookbook Company, Inc.*
Mail this form with your check to: **8332 Brush St., Huntington Beach, CA 92647**

Enclosed is my check for _____ book(s) at $10.95 each $_____.

Name _____

Street _____

City _____ State _____ Zip _____